BUILDING CHURCH

practical wisdom for all church builders

STEPHEN MATTHEW

RIVER
PUBLISHING

River Publishing & Media Ltd
Barham Court
Teston
Maidstone
Kent
ME18 5BZ
United Kingdom

info@river-publishing.co.uk

Unless otherwise indicated, all Scripture quotations are taken from the NIV - Copyright © 1973, 1978, 1984 by Biblica

ISBN 978-1-908393-19-7

Printed and bound by CPI Group (UK) Ltd, Croydon, CR0 4YY

Contents

Acknowledgements

Where do I start?

This book is about Building Church, the "living stones" of which are the lives of real people. So I want to thank every person I have ever done church with, because this book is actually about you and our joint efforts to build a community that is worthy to be called "God's House".

But in particular I want to thank the Abundant Life Church in Bradford, Belfast and Leeds. You have been my "stone-mason's yard" and I count it a privilege that you have allowed me to hone my church-building skills with you. Together we have made God smile by building a truly bespoke expression of his church in the world.

Over 30 years of names now come to mind, all worthy of acknowledgement. Spiritual fathers and mentors, fellow leaders, friends and family, all of whom have worked with me and released me to be the person I am today. Thank you for believing in this builder.

Of them all I must thank three in particular: Keri Jones, my spiritual father and the one who first believed in me enough to give me a chance to become a church-builder. Paul Scanlon, my fellow-builder and friend, who has been a constant encouragement on the journey. And Kay, my wife and best friend, who has built alongside me every step of the way.

Thank you.

What Others Are Saying About Building Church

"I've worked with Stephen Matthew for over 30 years, and to say he loves the local church would be an understatement. People like him are a rare breed, but they bring a missing and much-needed insight to the global debate about how to build a relevant, contemporary local church whilst keeping her essence in tact.

My friend and I have probably dealt with every type of person and tackled every kind of situation imaginable during our years of building the church together, yet I have never once seen him become disillusioned with the process. His belief that the local church is the best idea God ever had, coupled with his steady and tireless work to make that a reality, is what makes him the best guy I know to write this book. To its pages he brings not only his decades of experience, but also his continuing daily involvement in the trenches of local church life.

This is Stephen's journey and perceptions, and if I were you I'd listen to what he has to say. I have for over 30 years, and genuinely could not have achieved all I have without him alongside me. He is the most stable, consistent, unflappable person I've ever met – and when it comes to the rollercoaster ride that building the local church often is, that stuff's just pure gold. Every local church leadership team needs the wisdom of a Stephen Matthew and this book now makes that a little more possible."
Paul Scanlon, Senior Pastor, Abundant Life Ministries

"Church Builders - this could be the book you have been waiting for! When you want to learn from someone, you want to know they have wisdom, experience and a proven track record. Stephen Matthew is one of those people. What oozes from these pages is such a love for God's heart – His Church. 'Building Church' takes you on a thorough, step-by-step journey of how to take the seed of a vision to the realisation of a vibrant, dynamic and growing church. Without prescribing a model, Stephen unpacks biblical principles with very practical application giving understanding, insight and the tools to equip you to translate them into the context you are in. Within only a few pages this comprehensive study covers the breadth and depth of what's involved in building church and how to navigate the unique vision you are living for.

Stephen is part of the senior leadership of Abundant Life Church, where these principles are being lived out. As a result it has become an outstanding example of how to develop a church with a strong spiritual dynamic and life, coupled with very fruitful and transformational outreach in a community and city."
Clive Urquhart, Senior Pastor, Kingdom Faith Church

"Stephen has written a highly valuable resource for everyone who loves church. His observations are born out of years of faithful and successful ministry in a ground breaking setting. This is not mere theory, but a practical help for anyone desiring to build church in the 21st century."
Stuart Bell, Senior Pastor of New Life Lincoln and Leader of the Ground Level network.

"With a teacher's clarity and a pastor's passion – and the authenticity of a very down-to-earth human being – Stephen Matthew shares with us the exciting, exacting and ultimately enriching journey a local church can take in becoming all that it is intended to be. I know Stephen and his desire to equip leaders for greater effectiveness shines through the pages of this warm, well-constructed and very enlightening book. Every church leader, or potential church leader, who aspires to build the church of a lifetime should read this book."
Mal Fletcher, Chairman 2020Plus, London

"The most effective, pervasive, God-birthed and transformational institution on the planet, bar none, is the Church of the Lord Jesus Christ. It reaches into the most populated or the sparsest regions of our globe. There it is changing lives, communities and human destiny. Stephen's book, rooted in deep personal experience and strong biblical principle, practically demonstrates how to build that kind of dynamic, life-giving church in a local community. Pick it up, read it and these same truths will empower you to build with Jesus His Church."

Gary Skinner, Senior Pastor of Watoto Church, Kampala and founder of Watoto Childcare Ministries.

"This book is an honest, up-front, experience-based, practical tool about the greatest expression of God to the world, the Church! Stephen Matthew, through years of research and experience, has clearly articulated the many facets of how to do church really well. His clever way of making complex issues easy to grasp makes this book a must read. Do so and you will see your church in a new and completely different light."

Dr Scott Wilson, President Eurolead.net

"Stephen Matthew knows what he's talking about – he's been building church for over 30 years! Building Church is an unmissable book, precisely because Stephen is passing on his experience, not only from the past, but also from the present. Advice like that is worth its weight in gold, so I heartily commend this most helpful book. If you're a church leader, do yourself and your church a favour - read it!"

Revd. Rob White, Fresh Streams Network Minister and Chairman of Hope for Justice

Introduction

Building is in my blood. I love it and will be doing it until the day I die!

Just how it got there took me a while to understand, because I was not raised in a traditional building environment. I had wonderful, godly parents but they were not the practical kind when it came to hands-on building.

My Dad had soft hands from working in the office environment of a small engineering company and Mum was a homemaker. The only time I ever saw a builder during my childhood was when one was called in to do repairs to our home. Back in the 1960s, DIY had not been invented and I don't think my Dad even owned a tool kit!

It was strange, then, that my first-ever job was labouring in a builders merchant's yard. It was only meant to be a short-term thing between school and university, where I planned to study law. But the longer I lingered there, the more it got into my blood.

I loved the smell of the freshly sawn timber which I spent hours sorting and loading onto customers' trucks. I soon became familiar with the qualities of a wide range of both hard and soft woods and took great pleasure from their texture, form and construction potential. I still love that smell! Then there was the amazing variety of pipes and couplings in the plumbing and drainage section, the concrete products, the wide range of bricks, tiles, paving slabs and the endless bags of sand and gravel we had to shovel.

But best of all was the tool section. I spent ages browsing the tools, fascinated by their gleaming edges and pondering their intended purpose. There is something wonderful about a well-made tool; it is a joy to handle and to use. Of course, I had to have some of them, not that I had a use for them at that stage of my life. But there I started my tool collection. Going to work was a pleasure; I got to handle all the elements of what seemed to me to be one big construction kit.

That job only lasted seven months but it contributed to a major change in the direction of my life. By the end of that period I had decided to drop doing law: rather than go to university I joined a local surveying practice and became a trainee chartered surveyor, studying for my professional exams by extension and day release.

It took me five and a half years to qualify – which was fast by that route – but it was a great choice. Every day I got to mess with buildings! I bought, sold, leased, managed, valued, surveyed and analysed buildings and their construction. To this day I instinctively survey the fabric of every house I enter – which can be annoying!

The following few years were spent working my way up the profession and I am confident I could have enjoyed a long and rewarding career in the construction industry if I had remained in it. But life is bigger than any single job.

Through this whole period I had increasingly invested my spare time into building something else – the church. That too was instinctive; it was the way I had been raised. My parents had poured their lives into building the Brethren assembly I attended all my childhood, and modelled both faithfulness and courage by leading that small church through a total reinvention after the charismatic renewal of the early 1970s.

A new church was born and, freshly baptised in the Holy Spirit, I wholeheartedly threw all my spare time into helping build it. Those were heady days in which the church leadership began to empower and release a generation of young leaders, which included me and my new friend, Paul Scanlon. By 1982 Kay and I had a young, growing family and were fully immersed in the challenges of careers, family life and doing church.

Then the curve ball came! I was approached by the church leadership and invited to consider joining the staff as a full-time Pastoral Deacon – whatever that is! To cut a long story short, we decided to go for it. I reasoned that at twenty-six I was still young enough to give it a shot and if it didn't work out could always return to building surveying as long as I kept my credentials up to date.

But that was a massive decision. It changed everything, not least my building aspirations which I laid down, trusting God knew what he was doing as we followed his lead into this new adventure. The builder in me was set aside and a new main focus emerged: to pastor and lead the church. What a privilege.

At that stage, any relationship between my love for the church and my love for building was lost on me. What I now realise is that God simply took a man with a passion to build and directed those talents into building the most important house on the planet – his house. It was a simple fulfilment of the principle explained by the apostle Paul where he says, "first the natural, then the spiritual" (1 Corinthians 15:46, paraphrased).

The natural builder was becoming a spiritual builder. But it took a while for that penny to drop and for me to understand what God was playing at, because I still loved building and buildings. At the time it felt as if I was throwing away all those years of study and experience for the sake of leading the church. What I now know is that with God, nothing is wasted.

About a year into my full-time ministry, the church's recently appointed eldership and staff went on a retreat to team-build, pray and plan for the forthcoming period. Memorably, it was the first such event I had ever been on. We were still trying to get to know each other and work out how we would best function together, so it was all just a bit tense. And to make matters worse, we had no senior pastor at that time; we were deemed to be equals, so we all sat back and waited for someone to take the lead. More tension!

To break the ice, someone decided it would be good for us to read the book of Nehemiah together and discuss what we found there – and it changed my life. We spent two days reading and sharing; I devoured it over and over again. Why? Because Nehemiah was a builder. To this day I love that book, and its principles inform so much of what I do as a church builder. I now realise God was graciously unlocking the builder in me for his higher purpose. But I still didn't fully see it at the time.

Some years later I sat with Keri Jones, one of my formative spiritual fathers, pondering my next steps. I had served at Abundant Life Church, Bradford for eight years, then relocated to the Midlands to serve the apostolic team of ministries we worked with. That four-year season had involved travelling to minister in churches across the UK and Europe, obtaining my theological qualifications and becoming principal of the movement's Bible College.

I was now wrestling with a range of issues – not least that I was approaching 40 and needed to be sure I was doing the right thing for the rest of my life. I loved what I did – teaching, training, discipleship, networking, writing, organising – but not the itinerant context I did it in. Keri skilfully sent me back to God and the things God had spoken to me about. When I returned to see him I had just one scripture ringing in my heart: "You will be called Repairer of Broken Walls, Restorer of Streets with Dwellings" (Isaiah 58:12).

The builder in me was still aching to get out! The subsequent conversations helped me realize that I was not interested in itinerant ministry for its own sake; I was a "builder," not a "blesser." I needed to remain somewhere long enough to get something built, then from that secure base I could help other builders make repairs to their walls. One thing was clear though: the current season was over and we needed to move on.

The next three years were some of the most exciting and challenging of our life. We left the security of apostolic team ministry and followed God's leading to Lancaster in the North West of England where I returned to building surveying three days a week and continued to do ministry the rest of the time as opportunities arose. We got stuck into building a great local church in the city but without any leadership position. Slowly the fog cleared and, supported by Keri and others, God graciously guided us back to our home city of Bradford and a reunion with Paul Scanlon and the Abundant Life Church. We were older, wiser, more secure in who we were and best of all, ready to build.

I immediately threw myself into refreshing the church's pastoral structure, small group system and discipleship programmes – all familiar territory to me. But what lay ahead was not. By late 1998 as a church we had been released from our historic apostolic network and become an independent ministry. We had launched into a building programme to construct a 2000-seat auditorium on our campus, which was due for completion in the year 2000. The ground had also been prepared to launch our church-based Leadership Academy – one of my greatest loves in life!

Then one day Paul walked into my office. As we looked out across the car park from my office to the steel frame that was emerging from the ground just 100 meters away, he said, "God's been talking to me about what we are doing and this building project. And we are not simply moving our existing church into new premises; we are going to build a whole new church there."

Bemused, I asked for more information. And over the following days we began to understand that God was calling us to totally reinvent our church, to repurpose it, to rebuild it from top to bottom – and then establish that new church in our new building across the car park.

What happened next is Paul's story to tell and is well documented in his book *Crossing Over*.[1] I commend it to you. Every church leader guiding their church through transition needs to read that book. It is a church builder's book.

I now reflect back on the most eventful twelve years of my life in church building terms. It has been my absolute joy – though also pain at times – to help build the Abundant Life Church. We grew from a church of hundreds to a church of thousands. We deliberately turned from being a good, stable but rather inward-looking church and became an outreach station. We now exist for one purpose: to reach the lost, establish those new believers in a great church, equip them, and then release them to reach more lost people. That is our cycle of life.

The new church we built gradually became a resource to the wider body of Christ. Through our conferences, Leadership Academy, community outreach initiatives, network of churches, media products, books, CDs, music and worship, many more have been inspired and helped to build in their local communities. The "sound of the house" we built has been taken around the world – and to this day it humbles me that God allowed me to contribute to its success.

What follows in this book are many of the lessons I have learned from that process. I write not as the senior pastor but as his associate and friend, as a team player who simply brought his skill-set to the table to be used in harness with those of others. I certainly did not and could not have done any of this alone. So credit for what follows is shared.

Why write it at all? Because I am a builder and "repairer of broken walls." I now realise that God put my love for building in me; it is part of the essential me and needs to be shared with others. And God has impressed upon me, through the encouragement of faithful friends, that others could be helped to build churches in their communities from the lessons we learned together at

Abundant Life. So, if I have a building tool I can give you, it is yours to keep for the sake of the kingdom and in fulfilment of my passion to build God's house.

Funnily enough, I am still building buildings too. Every church I have been in since entering full-time ministry in 1982 has undertaken building projects – who says God doesn't have a sense of humour? Inevitably, I was invited onto the team assisting the spiritual leaders in each place we have lived: Bradford, Leicester and Lancaster. I have now project-managed all three buildings on our present campus at a total build cost of over £6 million.

It has also been my joy to advise and support many other church leaders undertaking building projects through a process which is often unique – banks, builders and construction people rarely understand churches, and churches can be a nightmare client for those respected professionals. So you see, nothing is wasted with God. I love it!

When God instructed his distracted people to get on with building the temple in Haggai's day, he said, "Go up into the mountains and bring down timber and build the house, so that I may take pleasure in it and be honoured" (Haggai 1:8). This teaches us two things: first, that building God's house will be hard work – climbing mountains to cut down trees, then shaping them into construction timber is just like reaching lost people and shaping their lives for Christian service. Then it shows that the finished product should be a house God takes pleasure in and is honoured by. That's a challenge, but of the kind builders love.

My prayer is that this book will help you to build the church in a way that brings a smile to God's face. As he surveys all you do, every worship service, outreach, act of kindness, prayer meeting, media clip, announcement, small group, piece of literature, building project, message that's preached, class that's taught, across every department of church life – he will feel honoured and derive great pleasure from it. It is our life's work: Building Church.

Section 1:
Guiding Principles

The Church Everyone Wants To Build

Chapter 1

The Church Everyone Wants To Build:

"I'd Love To Build A Church Like That."

"Wow! I'd love to be in a church like this!" Surely every Christian, and certainly every church leader, has said that at least once in their life and probably many times.

I vividly remember my first time. It was February 1980 and I was just 24. By then I was married and we were expecting our second child. I had qualified as a chartered surveyor and was enjoying the early challenges of climbing the professional ladder. We were also totally involved in our local church; we loved it. We were by then regional leaders, which meant we brought oversight and direction to a number of small groups in our area of the city. I spoke from time to time in church, served wherever I was needed and was classically what we would today call an "emerging leader."

My older brother David worked full time on the pastoral leadership of the church and was also the principal of our denomination's newly-established Bible School. As such, he got to travel to churches outside of our immediate network, a world I knew very little about at that stage of my Christian church awareness. So, it was a landmark day when he asked if I would fancy accompanying him on a ministry trip to the USA. I nearly fell off my chair! What an opportunity to see the world and what God was doing out there.

Money was my only hesitation, as I knew there was no way the church would be paying for me to go. But being the thoughtful brother he is, David had already talked about it with our dad who had agreed to fund me. I am forever grateful for a godly father who generously supported all his children in their pursuit of serving the Lord.

So on a freezing, snowy February day I entered what was then called Bible Temple in Portland, Oregon, and found myself uttering those words: "Wow! I'd love to be in a church like this!" We were generously hosted by Pastor Dick Iverson and his team and had a thoroughly great time.

What made the deepest impact was the sheer scale of it all. There were 1,400 people in church that weekend and I was used to 300 being a packed house! The church premises were superb by our standards, built for purpose and modern. The whole place amazed me. It opened my eyes to new possibilities and enlarged the sphere of my thinking about what church could look like today. A seed was sown.

What's more, they had a Bible School on the campus – the main reason we were there from David's point of view – which was a whole new concept to me. A Bible School based in a church? How odd. Little did I know that 20 years later I would be launching the Abundant Life Leadership Academy – in essence, a church-based Bible School. I tell you, absolutely nothing is wasted with God. That seed took a long time to germinate in me but God knew exactly what he was doing when he subtly sowed it into my spiritual subconscious all those years ago.

That trip changed my life on so many fronts. It exposed me to a model of church that was awe inspiring to me and made me say repeatedly to myself: "I'd love to build a church like that."

Since those formative days I have had the joy of visiting other churches around the world and laboured as a church-builder myself for 30 years. Many times I have said "Wow!" to myself and pressed leaders of churches far larger than mine for the secrets of their success.

In more recent years, God graciously allowed me to be on the other side of that question as the Abundant Life Church began to attract attention from other church-builders from around the world. I've lost count of the conference delegates, pastors and leaders who, having seen some aspect of how we are building church today, asked, "How did you build this church?"

The question is flattering, of course, but it's wise to be cautious how you answer it! Why? Because there is no single key to building a thriving church. In fact maybe the best answer to the question is to say, "I don't know! All we did was walk in obedience to Christ, one step at a time, making bold decisions and reaching lost people." That has actually become our stock answer and it is the absolute truth.

Enduring principles

A great church is built by taking many hundreds of small steps, not by turning a few large keys. So looking back and tracing the journey to extract the principles and dynamics that make any church what it is today, is a challenge. But that is the challenge I have set myself in writing this book.

I do remain convinced that there are enduring principles of church building we can learn from the Scriptures and from each other as church-builders, as long as we do not try to simply copy one another. This is therefore a book about church building principles that I believe can work anywhere. I have seen them applied in countries and cultures as diverse as the world is today – in first, second and third-world environments – as well as across all sectors of British and European society.

But before we can usefully turn to the guiding principles, you must settle it for yourself once and for all: there is no transferable model of building church. It is that simple. All off-the-shelf models are doomed to frustration and failure. There are no copies; every church is an original. How exciting is that!

Building church is a bespoke affair. It requires intimate knowledge of a wide range of locally variable elements, not least the unique blend of individual people you have the privilege of building into a thriving church community. Then add to that the context you are building in – its demography, prevailing socio-economic conditions, spiritual climate and cultural attitudes. Then you must add the physical resources at your disposal such as buildings – or lack of them – and other assets.

To that, add the gift-based resources within your people: do you have gifted musicians, dancers, prayer warriors, children's workers, youth workers, administrators, people who love the elderly, homeless, recovering addicts, prisoners, business leaders ... or a room full of spectators? As a leader you have to build with what you've got, and the variables are so diverse it makes your building unique.

As Pastor Tommy Barnett has powerfully written and articulated, *There's a miracle in your house*. If you have never heard him preach this message or read his book of the same name, get it today.[2]

He says:

"Pastors need to realise that everything they need to build a great church is already in their congregations ... in your house God has already planted the seeds that can blossom and become the answer to your most desperate dilemma... Life is everywhere, lying dormant, just waiting to come forth. Tiny seeds waiting to become something great... I believe everyone has the seed in them to do something great for God. I believe it even when I can't see it. I know there's a miracle in there somewhere."

It takes faith to believe that with the "living stones" at your disposal right now, you can build a great church. Yet that is the challenge. It is what drives church-builders to craft a community of believers that is unique, truly itself, not a copy, but a bespoke construction that glorifies its divine builder, Jesus.

So the best I can offer in this book are principles, not a transferable blueprint. And if you are ever offered something that promises to be one, reject it as faulty goods!

Having said all that, God presents the church in the New Testament to us in such a way that we must say to ourselves, "I'd love to build a church like that!" Inevitably, we then ask, "How did they do it?" and try to copy it. It is hard to copy the first-century church because we are the twenty-first century church and so many of the variables we work with are vastly different, but the underlying principles do remain the same. So if we can isolate and carefully apply them into our individual settings, we all have the potential to build "the church everyone wants."

I am sure that like me, you have explored the Bible on this theme. The more I do so, the more it confirms my point. In his wisdom God gave us a set of church-building principles, not a one-size-fits-all pattern to apply. It is those principles, applied with skill and wisdom into your unique church-building context that now determines your ultimate success or failure.

Let's take a closer look at what they are. This is the groundwork, the foundation-laying exercise that underpins every significant church you will ever encounter today. So, if you are serious about playing your part in building a thriving church in your community, you must fully grasp what comes next!

Chapter 2

The Church Everyone Wants To Build:
The Pictures

To this day, my heart races when I read the first few chapters of Acts! It draws from me a passion to build something like that early church in my generation. "If only our church was like that ..." Well, I have become convinced it can be. Stick with me as I explain.

God presents the New Testament church to us in two ways: in pictures and in action.

• The *pictures* are a set of simple metaphors which collectively teach us what the church is: its essential nature.
• The *action* is found in the vivid accounts and stories which describe the church at work in society, doing its God-appointed thing.

From these pictures and stories of the church in action we derive our essential ecclesiology – what we believe about the nature and purpose of the church. From those beliefs flow our methods and patterns of building church today.

It is not now my intention to take you on a detailed study through the various pictures used to describe the church in the Bible; it will be far more profitable if you do it yourself. But here are a few in brief outline to show you what I mean and to provoke you to have a serious look at what these and all the other pictures of the church teach us.

One thing I would say, though: if you do not take the trouble to personally grasp the guiding principles encapsulated in these simple, God-given pictures, you will never truly build God's house in the way he intended. As a result, what you build will not actually be God's house; it will be your house, whatever name you decide to stick on it. And what you build, you have to sustain. But when we build God's house according to his guiding principles and on the biblical foundation he has given us, he will build with us. Only then do we succeed in constructing a church where God is honoured and in which he takes pleasure (Haggai 1:8).

Jesus said, "I will build my church" (Matthew 16:18). So we are only ever co-labourers with Christ at best. We must therefore deeply grasp and love with a passion the guiding principles he has given us to build with, which are encapsulated in these wonderful pictures.

Bricks and mortar

The church is pictured as a building in the Scriptures: not any old building, but the building God lives in. The church is God's house.

God's desire to live in and among his people permeates the Bible narrative from beginning to end. In Genesis we read that God spoke to people from heaven. In Exodus he descended to a mountain top and spoke to Moses from there, and by the close of the book he inhabited the tabernacle around which the whole community of God's people camped (Exodus 40:24-38). This process teaches us that God took the initiative to dwell among his people, providing animal sacrifice to cover their sin lest they perish in the presence of his holiness.

The temple in Jerusalem became God's more permanent dwelling place, replacing the mobile tabernacle. All the feasts and festivals took God's people there, to be where God was. The great psalms of pilgrimage flowed out of their desire to be where God dwelt, with words which still inspire modern Christians to draw close to God. Words like:

"How lovely is your dwelling-place, O Lord Almighty! My soul yearns, even faints, for the courts of the Lord; my heart and my flesh cry out for the living God."

"Blessed are those who dwell in your house; they are ever praising you. Blessed are those whose strength is in you, who have set their hearts on pilgrimage… They go from strength to strength, till each appears before God in Zion."

"Better is one day in your courts than a thousand elsewhere; I would rather be a doorkeeper in the house of my God than dwell in the tents of the wicked." (Psalm 84:1-2, 4-5, 7, 10)

The ultimate expression of God dwelling among his people is seen in the coming of Christ to live in human form and die for our sins, and then after defeating death, sending his Spirit to dwell in every individual who puts their faith in him. Hence Paul says, "Your body is a temple of the Holy Spirit, who is in you, whom you have received from God" (1 Corinthians 6:19), and Peter makes the point that collectively we are now "like living stones…being built into a spiritual house" (1 Peter 2:5). The church is God's house.

The power is in our connectedness and inter-relatedness. No stone alone constitutes a house; it is made up of many. And this is our challenge as church-builders: to take the unique "living stones" represented by individual Christians and build them together into a construction that glorifies God, motivated by a conviction that, "In him the whole building is joined together and rises to become a holy temple in the Lord. And in him you too are being built together to become a dwelling in which God lives by his Spirit" (Ephesians 2:21-22).

The picture of the church as a building abounds with lessons about who we are as God's people. Each stone is needed, but finds its place in being connected to others. That process will involve being shaped by the divine stonemason. The stones all stand on the same foundation for stability and together constitute an expression of God's desire to dwell among people who willingly love and obey him. The church is God's address in every community across the world today, making him accessible for all to see. That's what we are building!

Urban living

Just as the Old Testament building God dwelt in is a picture of the church today, so is the city it was located in. Jerusalem, Mount Zion, the City of the Great King, and the Mountain of the Lord's House are just some of the frequently used terms to describe the city where God lived.

The point here is that wherever God dwelt, around him developed a God-centred community which became an expression of his life. Here are people living under his benevolent rule, a distinct, ordered society which was so observably blessed that nations would look on and say, "Come, let us go up to the mountain of the Lord, to the house of the God of Jacob. He will teach us his ways, so that we may walk in his paths" (Isaiah 2:3).

God's people, Israel, were supposed to be a "light for the Gentiles" (Isaiah 49:6), a mandate that carries through to the church today.

Of us Jesus said, "You are the light of the world. A city on a hill cannot be hidden" (Matthew 5:14).

The church is a city, a city on a hill, which can be seen from miles around and towards which people are attracted. Cities have form and structure; they are ordered communities with clear governance and laws regulating the life of their citizens. Ancient cities had walls and gates so it was evident who was a citizen and who was not. A city is made up of many interwoven streets, housing many different trades and professions, each an expression of city life. There are households within the larger city where everyone can feel at home, be safe and contribute to the welfare of the city as a whole.

These and other lessons abound when you start thinking of building a church that is like a city. The book of Ezra comes alive when you meditate on the church being a building, or more specifically, the temple. The lessons Nehemiah learned when rebuilding the devastated walls of Jerusalem are mirrored in many a modern church-builder's efforts to rebuild or repair churches devastated by the enemies of sin, divisiveness and poor leadership. Some of these we will reflect on later in this book.

Another fascinating city-based study to consider is the relationship between the two central cities in the Bible: Jerusalem and Babylon. Jerusalem is the centre of godliness and Babylon the centre of wickedness and all that is opposed to God. Enough said.

In short, we are building a spiritual Jerusalem, a city whose community expresses all that God is. It is to that city we came when we came to Christ, as the Hebrew writer enthuses: "You have come to Mount Zion, to the heavenly Jerusalem, the city of the living God. You have come to … the church of the firstborn, whose names are written in heaven" (Hebrews 12:22-23).

In this imagery, so many pictures converge around the central thought that God lives in a city, which today is called the church. That community, that city, that church is what we are building and who wouldn't want to come and live with us there?

Bride and groom

Christianity is not a religion; it is a relationship between God and his people. It is a deeply personal, loving relationship like that between two lovers, best pictured as a bride and groom who enthusiastically enter a life-long commitment to unconditionally love one another and be together. That is how we each feel about our relationship with Jesus. But it is also a corporate relationship, because all of us who love Jesus are united in our shared love for him.

Throughout the Old Testament God speaks of his people in the warm and tender terms of a marriage relationship. He is the groom, they are the bride. He chose his bride and entered into a relationship of covenant love with her; the marriage was formalised. But sadly, his Old Testament people committed spiritual adultery by worshipping other gods and forsaking their one true love. Breach of the marriage covenant resulted in all manner of trouble for unfaithful Israel.

Jeremiah writes, "Have you seen what faithless Israel has done? She has gone up on every high hill and under every spreading tree and has committed adultery there" (Jeremiah 3:6). As a result, God issued a certificate of divorce to her (Jeremiah 3:8). Through Ezekiel God uses the same analogy to describe the breakdown of his relationship with his people: "They committed adultery with their idols; they even sacrificed their children, whom they bore to me, as food for them" (Ezekiel 23:37), revealing just how deeply God feels about idolatry and the way Israel had strayed at that time.

Their unfaithfulness led to their eventual exile to Babylon, the city that represents all that is against God. But God is good and his love for his bride remained despite their sin, as seen in the book of Hosea, which is an extended analogy about God's willingness to forgive and re-marry his adulterous wife.

Again, all these pictures reach their ultimate fulfilment in the New Testament. Jesus came to earth for the sake of his bride, the Church. Paul writes, "Christ loved the church and gave himself up for her to make her holy, cleansing her by the washing with water through the word, and to present her to himself as a radiant church, without stain or wrinkle or any other blemish, but holy and blameless" (Ephesians 5:25-27).

Jesus taught that when the end comes and we are united with him in heaven forever, it will be initiated by the wedding supper of the Lamb (Revelation 19:9). Until then, the church is like a bride making herself ready for the big day! A prepared bride looks radiant, and is pure, holy and undivided in her love for her groom. The lessons abound, challenging us to build a church that increasingly looks like the most beautiful bride we have ever seen. That's what we are building.

And such is the wonderful tapestry of Scripture that all these pictures are woven together like multicoloured threads in passages that anticipate the culmination of the church's union with Christ when he returns again and we are united with him forever:

"I saw the Holy City, the new Jerusalem, coming down out of heaven from God, prepared as a bride beautifully dressed for her husband. And I heard a loud voice from the throne saying, "Now the dwelling of God is with men, and he will live with them. They will be his people, and God himself will be with them and be their God." (Revelation 21:2-3)

Here we have all three pictures mentioned so far – the building, the city and the Bride – all woven together. That's what we are building!

Healthy body

"Now you are the body of Christ, and each one of you is a part of it," said Paul (1 Corinthians 12:27). The picture of the church being like a body is probably the best known and been the most used analogy by church-builders over the centuries. It is simple, clear and powerful.

In a body every part is needed. Some parts are seen and others hidden, but visibility is not a measure of importance. It is ridiculous for one part of a body to think it does not need another part or for it to feel inferior – we are what we are, and find fulfilment as we carry out the role within the body that we were created for. Read and meditate on 1 Corinthians 12 and let the lessons from this picture inform the kind of church you are building, because we all instinctively know as we read it that this is the kind of church we want.

Our essential oneness is mirrored in this picture. We are all one in Christ and every local expression of church is just a microcosm of the universal unity we share with every believer who has ever lived – the "universal church" as theologians call it. Our oneness is spiritual, based upon our each being in "Christ [who] is the head of the church, his body, of which he is the Saviour" (Ephesians 5:23). As a body we respond to the direction, voice and thoughts of our head, Jesus Christ.

This picture teaches us about our mutual interdependence, our individual importance to the health of the whole and the sheer impossibility of thriving as a believer outside of the Christian community. To be seen to be all that God intended it to be, the church must live, move and act as a unified body. That's what we are building!

Family life

"I am writing you these instructions so that … you will know how people ought to conduct themselves in God's household, which is the church of the living God" (1 Timothy 3:14-15). The church is God's household, his family, and just like all families it has a code of conduct, acceptable patterns of behaviour and a range of relationships for us to navigate.

The moment we are "born again" (John 3:3), we become part of the family of God. Not just as another child, lost among the millions who also call God their heavenly Father, but as a child intimately known, loved and adopted by our loving Father. Spiritually speaking we are all sons, whether male or female, which releases to us the full rights of sons (Galatians 4:5) who, under ancient biblical law, inherited the estate of the father and continued the family line.

Paul expands on this picture of the church in a number of places but nowhere better than in Galatians where he goes on to say, "Because you are sons, God sent the Spirit of his Son into our hearts, the Spirit who calls out, 'Abba, Father.' So you are no longer a slave, but a son; and since you are a son, God has made you also an heir" (Galatians 4:6-7).

Thinking through the picture of the church being a family gives us a context for nurturing, training, discipline and correction. In the family unit a child learns how to behave, to respect those who are older and wiser, and to eventually take responsibility for the younger ones in the family. The family is a multi-generational environment, a safe place to both weep and rejoice, and without doubt the most supportive environment that exists in the sphere of human relationships.

Into that family you and I were born, and as church-builders we must now construct our church relationships, fellowship and interaction in a way that affirms to everyone who joins the family through faith in Christ that they are "no longer foreigners and aliens, but fellow-citizens with God's people and members of God's household" (Ephesians 2:19). That's what we are building!

Shepherd and sheep

The shepherding picture is prominent in Scripture. From the Psalmist who famously said "The Lord is my shepherd, I shall not be in want" (Psalm 23), through to Jesus who declared himself to be "the good shepherd" (see John 10:11) and New Testament church leaders who are told to "keep watch over yourselves and all the flock of which the Holy Spirit has made you overseers. Be shepherds of the church of God, which he bought with his own blood" (Acts 20:28).

The church is like a flock of sheep. We have one shepherd who leads us to places where the grass is nourishing and refreshing water is always nearby. This good shepherd protects us from predators, wolves in sheep's clothing, and always guards the door of the sheepfold. He will even lay his life down for his sheep and go the extra mile to bring back ones that stray.

This picture has much to teach us about the nature of the church as a community, its pastoral culture and structures, its benefits, responsibilities and the way to promote health within the flock. This is what we are building!

Stop and ask...

These pictures are so simple that we can easily give them a nod of assent but never let the truth they are designed to communicate ever drop into our motivational centre, our heart. So before rushing on, just take a moment to reflect on the church you are helping to build in your community today. Think about the people, the leaders, the challenges you face, and see each picture there. Can you spot it?

Extract and highlight the guiding principles God has put within each picture. Grasp their importance because each is vital. Then proactively apply them to your personal church-building endeavours.

Is the church you are helping to build like...

A building, where each "living stone" is:

- Being shaped for their ideal place in the construction
- Built upon and in line with the foundation we all share
- Held in place by adjacent stones and the shared mortar of Christ
- Fully utilised and interconnected

A city, which is:

- Well governed and organised
- A safe place
- A place of opportunity
- A vibrant, attractive community
- A great environment to live

A bride, who is:

- Madly in love with her groom, Jesus
- Totally groom-centred
- Faithful to her groom
- Motivated to action by a desire to honour and obey her groom
- Being prepared for the "wedding day"

A body, that has:

- Every part functioning in a healthy way
- Interdependence – because no part can survive alone
- Interrelatedness – because life flows between us
- Unity – because we have a single form
- A clear direction, that comes from the head
- A distinct voice, whoever is the speaker

A family, where:

- All generations harmoniously work together
- There is training for life in a safe, secure environment
- Nurture, support and discipline are normal and expected
- Guests are always welcome
- Babies are regularly born

A flock, that is:

- Guided by the one good shepherd
- Cared for by under-shepherds with the good shepherd's heart
- Well fed and nourished
- Protected from predators

If we can flesh out just these six pictures, our churches will be compelling communities expressing God's life to the world. But there are more!

The full picture album

I am sure you are getting my point by now. God has not given us a drawing and said "Build the church exactly like this." Instead he has given us these wonderfully simple, accessible pictures to be our guiding principles and then expects us to work with him in a process to flesh them out in our unique contexts. That is the skill of the church-builder.

There are many more pictures but it is through exploring them as a personal study that they will reap you maximum benefit. There is nothing like studying the nature of the church you have a passion to build in the company of just the Bible and the Holy Spirit. In those times of exploration you will gain a deep revelation about the true nature of the church and divine wisdom about how to implement the guiding principles in your unique local community.

It is fascinating that not even the most celebrated theologians of the last few hundred years can agree on just how many of these pictures there actually are. Much depends on whether you take a purely New Testament view or whether, as I have done above, take a broad biblical view of images which are used to describe the people of God through both Testaments.

I believe that is the only way to get the full picture because whilst all the Old Testament types and picture are fulfilled in the

New, in many cases they are better described and illustrated by Old Testament pictures and stories than their New Testament counterparts. Never forget that the community of God's people – which we call the church – existed long before the New Testament and is pictured in God's dealings with Israel, the Old Testament people of God. So you need to do a study of the whole Bible, not just the New Testament, to get the full picture. I like to think of it as browsing the full picture album!

That's where books like Ezra and Nehemiah come alive to the modern church-builder, as well as the many wonderful pictures used by the Old Testament prophets to instruct God's people. The truth is, "All Scripture is God-breathed and is useful for teaching, rebuking, correcting and training in righteousness, so that the man of God may be thoroughly equipped for every good work" (2 Timothy 3:16-17). And if you want to build the church with skill and wisdom today, you need that thorough equipping that only comes from a working knowledge of the whole Word of God.

In his landmark book, *Images of the Church in the New Testament,*[3] Paul S. Minear presents one of the most comprehensive studies of the pictures of the church in print today. This scholarly and inspirational study identifies ninety-six such images, an indication of the breadth of language, metaphor, allegory and illustration used by the Bible writers to convey the essential nature of the Christian community.

Listing just a few more illustrates the diversity: the salt of the earth, a letter from Christ, branches of the vine, the elect lady, exiles, ambassadors, the light of the world, the holy temple, a royal priesthood, the new creation, fighters against Satan, the sanctified slaves, friends, sons of God, the disciples, the wearers of white robes. So, to fully grasp the essence of the church as communicated through the pictures of Scripture, read your Bible comprehensively so you have a full picture album to inform the way you build.

One final remark before we move on to explore the guiding principles seen in the "action" of the New Testament church. I ended each of my brief comments about the six pictures mentioned above by saying, "That's what we are building!" It struck me on each occasion that I was taking responsibility for doing something that Jesus said he would do.

You will recall that when Peter had his revelation of who Jesus was – "the Christ, the Son of the living God" (Matthew 16:16) – Jesus responded by saying that on the rock that was Peter and his revelation of Jesus, he would build something. He said, "I will build my church, and the gates of Hades will not overcome it" (Matthew 16:18). Jesus took ownership of the church; it is his, he died for it and he is fully committed to building it.

So we can be in peace. Our task is to build with Jesus for, as the psalmist says, "Unless the Lord builds the house, its builders labour in vain" (Psalm 127:1). So please understand, every time I use language which implies I, we or you are building the church, I always mean we are doing it fully in cooperation with God, the one who is "the builder of everything" (Hebrews 3:4).

So, the principles illustrated by all these pictures – the full picture album – are what we use to guide us as we build the church in our individual communities today. They are one half of our essential guiding principles. To the other we now turn.

Chapter 3

The Church Everyone Wants To Build:
The Action

The church of the scriptures is not primarily a structural organisation but a dynamic, many-faceted community, a living organic unity. Structure is present, order is vital and government essential, but never at the expense of the essential life of the church. For wherever structure impedes vitality, something is wrong. It is this wonderful ordered fluidity we read about in the earliest accounts of the New Testament church.

Without reading the whole New Testament, let me illustrate my point from just four passages in the early chapters of Acts. These are what I call "window passages" because they appear as short descriptions of the church in action between the main events of the storyline. It is as if Luke steps back from the incidents and characters of his main story line to give us a glimpse of the big picture, the overriding ethos and essential dynamics that characterised the church within which and through whom they took place. When I read these "window passages," my heart cries out to God, "help me to build a church like that!" Here they are in full:

"They devoted themselves to the apostles' teaching and to fellowship, to the breaking of bread and to prayer. Everyone was filled with awe at the many wonders and signs performed by the apostles. All the believers were together and had everything in common. They sold property and possessions to give to anyone who had need. Every day they continued to meet together in the temple courts. They broke bread in their homes and ate together with glad and sincere hearts, praising God and enjoying the favour of all the people. And the Lord added to their number daily those who were being saved." (Acts 2:42-47)

"All the believers were one in heart and mind. No one claimed that any of their possessions was their own, but they shared everything they had. With great power the apostles continued to testify to the resurrection of the Lord Jesus. And God's grace was so powerfully at work in them all that there were no needy persons among them. For from time to time those who owned land or houses sold them, brought the money from the sales and put it at the apostles' feet, and it was distributed to anyone who had need." (Acts 4:32-35)

"The apostles performed many signs and wonders among the people. And all the believers used to meet together in Solomon's Colonnade. No one else dared join them, even though they were highly regarded by the people. Nevertheless, more and more men and women believed in the Lord and were added to their number. As a result, people brought the sick into the streets and laid them on beds and mats so that at least Peter's shadow might fall on some of them as he passed by. Crowds gathered also from the towns around Jerusalem, bringing their sick and those tormented by impure spirits, and all of them were healed." (Acts 5:12-16)

"Day after day, in the temple courts and from house to house, they never stopped teaching and proclaiming the good news that Jesus is the Messiah." (Acts 5:42)

These passages have inspired many sermons, lectures and books. I am sure you will agree that this is the church we all want. But how can we get there? Once again we are presented with a description that offers us guiding principles rather than hard and fast patterns to copy. Here are dynamics to emulate, to aspire to, and to talk with God about.

On reflection, I believe we are here presented with the features of a healthy church in action; that's why we love these passages so much and want to reproduce what we read. So, over my years of church-building I have extracted from these passages fourteen features, which, I humbly suggest, should be present in any healthy church. They are the norms of New Testament church life against which we can to some extent assess our modern church's health. So, if nothing else it gives us the basis of a Church Health Check!

The important matter of how to then improve your church's health where it seems to be poor or lacking in these features, is the core skill of building church which we will come to in due course. But first, let's isolate the specific actions expressed in these four passages, actions which we could describe as the features of a healthy church in action:

1. They were individually devoted

"They devoted themselves..." (Acts 2:42)
This statement implies that each believer was personally devoted to growing in their relationship with God and playing their part in building a vibrant church. They were self-starters and self-builders. They epitomised Jude's exhortation to "build yourself up in your most holy faith" (Jude 20).

Each person took responsibility for "continuing steadfastly" (NKJV) in the disciplines that follow this opening statement. They did not just sit back and wait to be told what to do by the church leaders; they put themselves in, took initiative, and did the work of reaching the lost and building those people into a community.

When people give the gift of their devotion to the church leaders, the leaders can lead, facilitate, resource and direct that passion for Christ and his kingdom. It makes leadership a joy and not a burden. This fundamental attitude is the fuel for every growing church and at the core of every thriving church you will find a group of people like this – individually devoted to Jesus and becoming more like him.

2. The Bible was read, taught and outworked

"They devoted themselves to … the apostles' teaching." (Acts 2:42) Their devotion to the apostles' teaching means they listened eagerly to it being communicated, read it once it was committed to writing, and eagerly applied it to their lives. That same teaching of the early apostles of Christ is enshrined for all time in the New Testament. So our modern equivalent is to have a church of people who love God's Word, read their Bibles, and love to hear it communicated, expounded and applied. Then with single-minded devotion, they live it out to the full.

A church of people individually rooted in the Bible is a force to be reckoned with! They are a people of faith, because faith springs from believing that Word. They are a people who think, speak and act like Jesus because just as he was "the word made flesh," they now flesh out God's enduring word to mankind revealed through those same Scriptures.

They are people of the light, who understand how God thinks and feels about the world and the people in it. They truly represent his heart and embody Christ's life for all to see and embrace. They are the Body of Christ in action.

Every thriving, healthy church has at its core a devotion to the Bible and all it teaches.

3. They enjoyed fellowship with God and each other

"They devoted themselves to... fellowship." (Acts 2:42)

The early church understood the importance of fellowship. In the modern church this is often misunderstood and read as "they devoted themselves to attending church." Whilst this is legitimate, it is only a secondary expression of devotion to fellowship.

The primary devotion involved in the word "fellowship" as used in the Bible is fellowship with God. Do the study and you will see it for yourself. Of all the references to fellowship in the Bible, the vast majority refer to our fellowship with God the Father, the Holy Spirit and with Christ. Then from this fellowship flows our shared life with each other; one informs and directs the other. The apostle John makes it clear that "our fellowship is with the Father and with his Son, Jesus Christ" and that is the basis on which "we have fellowship with one another" (1 John 1:3, 7).

Unless people are walking in devoted fellowship with God, they will never successfully develop healthy, enduring relationships with people. Herein lies the reason for so many of the interpersonal issues that church leaders end up trying to support people through.

In a thriving church each individual is walking in close fellowship with God and that relationship creates a wonderful context for developing healthy human relationship at every level – from marriage and family relationships, to business partnerships, friendships of all kinds, casual acquaintances and befriending strangers.

4. They broke bread regularly

"They devoted themselves to... the breaking of bread." (Acts 2:42)

The breaking of bread, communion, Eucharist or covenant meal – whatever your particular church tradition calls it – features regularly in healthy churches. The early church's devotion to breaking bread was probably a feature of their home-based gatherings (Acts 2:46) rather than their large celebrations where teaching, proclamation and worship would have been the main focus. When believers break bread they are taken right back to the roots of Christianity. The simple act of sharing bread and wine reminds us of Christ's death and the basis of our new life in him. It expresses our unity and takes us back to the simple truths of the faith. We are a redeemed people, saved by the shed blood of Jesus, graciously given a brand new start, an eternal hope and the ability to live life in all its fullness. These are truths we need to meditate on frequently when distracted by the razzmatazz of modern life and modern church. It is our essence.

A church that keeps the cross and the wonder of our salvation at its core by regularly facilitating and encouraging its people to break bread together will remain healthy and strong.

5. They were a praying people

"They devoted themselves... to prayer." (Acts 2:42)

The early Christians talked with God all the time. As they waited in the upper room for the Spirit to come after Christ's ascension, they prayed (Acts 1:14). When faced with threats and opposition, they prayed and the room shook (Acts 4:31)! As you read the book of Acts it is impossible to miss that they bathed everything they did in prayer as a natural expression of their intimate relationship with God. Healthy churches pray! And not just in an organised sense. Indeed, a personal devotion to involving God in every aspect of life through healthy conversation – prayer – always comes before a successful prayer meeting. If we have to call a prayer meeting to get people to pray, it will be hard work. But people who are personally devoted to prayer will instinctively find each other and gather to pray in a multitude of settings about a multitude of things without any pressure from church leaders.

6. The supernatural was evident

"Everyone was filled with awe at the many wonders and signs performed by the apostles" (Acts 2:43); *"People brought their sick ... and all of them were healed."* (Acts 5:12, 15-16)

It has often been said that the book of Acts is really about the acts of the Holy Spirit, rather than of the apostles. Of course both are true because the Holy Spirit dwells in and works through people.

Every incident of the main story line of Acts contains supernatural intervention: Pentecost (chapter 2), healing (chapter 3), buildings shaken (chapter 4), divine judgment and more healings (chapter 5) ... and so we can go on. It is not surprising, then, that the atmosphere of the church community was characterized by awe and genuine faith for God to intervene in a supernatural way. They were a naturally supernatural people. Healthy churches are Holy Spirit-led and have an ever-present anticipation that God will do what we cannot. We expect God to be present to convict, save, heal, restore and deliver every time we gather and in the flow of our everyday lives.

However modern and seeker-friendly our church services become in style and format, nothing must be allowed to replace our faith and expectation that God will perform signs and wonders among us today.

7. They enjoyed togetherness and a shared life

"All the believers were together and had everything in common." (Acts 2:44)

The early Christians were a genuine community, sharing with each other as appropriate (Acts 4:32) and characterised by a healthy togetherness. They identified with each other around their common faith in Christ and fleshed out the truth that the church community is not divided by "Jew nor Greek, slave nor free, male nor female" but is united in Christ, an all-inclusive body of believers (Galatians 3:28).

It would seem the early church quickly became an identifiable, alternative community characterised by its cohesion and shared life. The need for this is as apparent today as it was then. We live in a world which tends to encourage individuality, the pursuit of personal space and separateness rather than this kind of togetherness. But all human hearts crave to belong; God created us to be social beings and loneliness is still the scourge of humanity. In the face of this, healthy churches arise to demonstrate the community of the King! Thriving churches are places of inclusion, togetherness and shared life.

8. They held large and small gatherings
"...in the temple courts and from house to house." (Acts 5:42)
The early Christians "continued to meet together in the temple courts" and "they broke bread in their homes" (Acts 2:46). This pattern is seen throughout the New Testament and establishes a simple point – we need both large and small gatherings to best express and facilitate a healthy, growing church.

We need the large settings, the regular corporate celebrations, where we all come together for worship, teaching, proclamation and to express our love for a big God who has a large family. But it is easy to feel lost in the crowd, so we need smallness within the largeness, hence small groups based in homes, coffee shops, or other more relaxed informal settings. Healthy churches have both, and wise Christians fully involve themselves in both.

9. They were a praising people
"They continued to meet together ... praising God." (Acts 2:47)
Praise flows from gratitude. The first Christians understood just how amazing it is to be saved and free from the shackles of their former way of life. Their gatherings were therefore characterised by thanksgiving, gratitude and praise to God for all he has done. A healthy church is a place of praise and worship. Personal praise is

great but when we all come together to praise God, things happen! An attitude of praise lifts every situation to God and resolutely adopts his perspective on it. A praising church understands that God is awesome, our creator and source, our provider and redeemer, our saviour and king. A God-centred church will resound with praise, just because God is worthy of praise. Powerful praise is a feature found in all healthy, thriving churches.

10. They grew numerically

"More and more men and women believed in the Lord and were added to their number." (Acts 2:37; 5:14)

Every living thing grows. The church is no exception and the early church demonstrates this radically. After their increase from 120 to well over 3,000 souls following Peter's sermon at Pentecost, it just kept growing. By Acts chapter 6 we see the growth expressed as geographical spread too.

A lack of numerical church growth is often justified by claiming growth in depth or stature – statements like, we are growing in "quality not quantity." But it is inescapable: a healthy church is also a numerically growing church. For a church to exist for any other reason than to grow numerically immediately sets it on a course towards inward-looking self-destruction. Indeed, spiritual growth in quality should result in numerical growth in quantity, but where one is championed at the expense of the other, a dangerous imbalance results. Thriving churches are growing churches.

11. The fear of the Lord was present

"Everyone was filled with awe" (Acts 2:43) ... *"No one else dared join them ... Nevertheless, more and more men and women believed."* (Acts 5:13-14)

When Christians truly understand the nature of God, they can only bow in humble adoration. He defies description by mere words like "awesome," "magnificent" and "omnipotent." Nothing can describe the felt presence of God! In his holiness he resists all that oppose him; in his love and mercy he embraces all that call on his name. He is truly wonderful beyond description. The first Christians knew this, but the death of Ananias and Sapphira seriously sharpened their awareness of it (Acts 5:1-12). It inspired fear, but of the right kind: a reverential respect for God's holiness and right ways. Proverbs 16:6 says that "through the fear of the Lord a man avoids evil" and here is salutary evidence. The same God who heals, restores and intervenes through miracles, signs and wonders, is to be feared. When we get this balance right, we have a healthy church. All thriving churches have a healthy fear of the Lord permeating all they do.

12. They taught and proclaimed the gospel

"They never stopped teaching and proclaiming the good news." (Acts 5:42)

Teaching and preaching is what churches do! And based on the response to their efforts as recorded in Acts, they communicated exceptionally well. I believe all healthy churches communicate with credibility – because they are exemplifying what they preach – and with clarity. Their people know what they believe and why. There is no fog of confusion or waffle-filled messages that leave people as confused as when they arrived.

Healthy churches have leaders who work on their communication skills, honing their gift to better represent God's heart to the listeners. Whether they lead a small group or are senior pastor to multiple thousands, the principle holds good. In addition, they make use of modern media and every available practical resource to better communicate the glorious, timeless truth of the gospel to this generation. Note that they "taught and proclaimed" the gospel. Thriving churches enjoy both: teaching that clearly unpacks the faith line upon line, and preaching that proclaims the message in a way that propels us onwards to become all the Christ has called us to be. A healthy church enjoys a balanced diet of teaching and proclamation.

13. They enjoyed the favour of the community

"Enjoying the favour of all the people" (Acts 2:47); *"they were highly regarded by the people."* (Acts 5:13)

Christians should be the most conscientious and respected citizens wherever you find them in the world. We are the light, the salt, the tangible expression of Christ to the world, his body. And when we "go around doing good" (Acts 10:38) like Jesus did, most people will like us! There will of course always be evil people who hate the light that the gospel brings into society, but it seems that the goodness demonstrated by the early church endeared them to the majority of the community.

Healthy churches enrich the community they are building in. I love it when a church gets a reputation for helping people, doing good and being a net contributor to society. Favour flows from the community to those churches and people will go to those churches and find Christ. On the other hand, churches which fail to identify with the needs of their community and stand apart as islands of irrelevant spirituality tend to slowly die. A healthy church engages with and is, on balance, appreciated by its community.

14. They were a grace-filled community

"God's grace was so powerfully at work in them all." (Acts 4:33)

God's grace – his undeserved favour – was working in the lives of the early church. Grace was evident, not law, which characterised the Old Testament people of God. Healthy churches are grace-filled communities. We are individually saved by grace and now administer God's grace to one another (1 Peter 4:10).

It is noteworthy that when the gospel eventually reached the gentile territory of Antioch in Syria, Barnabas was sent to assess its genuineness. When he got there he looked for one thing, grace.

We read that when he "saw the evidence of the grace of God," he knew it was the real thing (Acts 11:23). Nothing compares to God's amazing grace, it is the evidence of God's power at work in our church community.

A healthy church is characterised by God's grace as opposed to legalistic law-keeping – however modern the laws!

So, there you have it! This brief survey of the early church in action reveals at least fourteen features for us to skilfully apply to our individual church-building contexts. I believe they all flowed from its healthy core and will therefore characterise healthy churches in every generation.

A health check tool

It is not uncommon that when visiting the church of a fellow pastor to minister in some capacity I am subsequently asked a question like, "Is there anything you think we could be doing better?" or "What are your overall observations about the church?" What comes next is very important.

On the one hand, who am I to make a comment about the way someone else is building their unique expression of church over the long-haul when I only have a snapshot to base my judgments on? Maybe it is best to say nothing at all. But on the other hand, they did ask! So maybe I should offer something, even if it's simply to encourage them in the building process. Pregnant pauses frequently follow questions such as these because we want to get it right.

Experience teaches that all the best advice and support for church-building flows from relationship and regular contact with the leaders and church in question. The level of relationship we have determines the quality of the conversations we will have during and after a visit, and the liberty we will each feel to make observations and constructive suggestions about our church-building efforts.

It took me a few years to realise that because I am a builder, I am best working with pastors consistently over a period rather than in one-off visits. But because the reality is I can only do that meaningfully with a few churches, I needed to think more creatively about how to visit a church once or twice and leave a significant building tool in their hands.

On one such occasion I was invited to speak at a church on the understanding that no one knew we were coming, so we could be the proverbial "secret shoppers" and give helpful feedback to the pastor. So my wife Kay and I were able to arrive as new faces, chat to the crowd and observe a whole range of things objectively. It was quite a shock to some when I then jumped up to preach!

But on most occasions this kind of input has been with the core leadership of the church in a more intimate setting. Some would call it consultancy but I have always thought that sounds far too pretentious. I regard it as helping fellow church-builders to construct a thriving church to truly represent our wonderful Lord and Saviour.

Over the years this process has consistently led me back to the simple pictures and accounts of the New Testament church in action we have considered above. That's because if I am asked to make a comment about the health of a church, I must first have a true awareness of what a healthy church looks like. And it is no good comparing your church with mine, however impressive you may think it is.

First, our respective churches are each unique expressions of building God's house and, second, who is to say my church is healthy by New Testament standards anyway? All church leaders are profoundly aware that their church is not perfect; we are always in process, under construction, on a journey, grappling with the dynamics of building God's house. So where does that leave us?

My response has been the development of a simple tool: a "church health check" based on the actions described earlier in this chapter. I first developed this after being invited to visit a church in the south-west of England to conduct a health check – their language, not mine, at the time. I had never been asked to do this so specifically before and so applied myself to the task.

What emerged for that occasion has since been refined into a church health check exercise. It consists of a simple set of questions and responses about aspects of church life. In truth, it is a totally unscientific way of assessing the health of a church. But if nothing else it generates healthy debate about aspects of church welfare that may otherwise be avoided to its overall detriment.

I offer it to you as an appendix. It is not meant to comprehensively sweep up every aspect of church life but it gets to the essence of the ingredients which combine to form a healthy church. Experience shows that it is of most help when the discussion is led by an objective observer – someone from outside the immediate church leadership team – and within the wider context of a discussion about your overall vision, mission, culture and structure, about which we will say more later in this book. I believe it will help any courageous leader to make a reasonably objective assessment of each aspect of their church's health, if it is discussed in an atmosphere of openness and complete honesty.

... and the rest

Before moving on from these guiding principles, which characterise "the church we all want to build," to more specifically exploring how to build "the church God wants you to build" in particular, I need to say one more thing.

To some, saying that the pictures and actions described above together constitute everything the New Testament gives us to build with in terms of guiding principles, may seem rather simplistic. Surely the New Testament has a lot more to say about how to build the church? And for those well versed in the Scriptures, texts will come to mind about a wide range of church-building matters addressed by the various New Testament authors. However, I would suggest that many of those texts in your mind are specific directives designed to keep a potentially wayward church on track. They are corrective commands, exhortations and encouragements to be the body, family, flock, holy temple and perfect bride we already are by virtue of our standing in Christ. They are in effect saying, "Be the pictures I have given to you as guiding principles." Similarly, many of the clear directives about how to conduct ourselves as the church are there to take us back to living out the actions we read about in Acts, where we all agree the church was in relatively good health.

For example, the writer to the Hebrews says, "Let us not give up meeting together, as some are in the habit of doing" (Hebrews 10:25), which is a clear directive to be at corporate church gatherings. Issued as a directive it can be a legalistic command used to get people to church out of a wrong sense of guilt, duty or fear. But when seen as an exhortation to be part of the church in action we read about in Acts, who met in both small and large gatherings for mutual benefit, worship, learning and encounters with God, it finds its true context.

Every text must be interpreted in its context – an important hermeneutical principle – but don't limit that context to just the book in question. Texts also have to be interpreted in the light of the whole of Scripture – the part interpreted in the light of the whole – for balance and soundness of doctrine to be developed. So it is legitimate to interpret a range of directives in the New Testament in the wider context of the New Testament images of the church and the accounts of that church in action.

Is not Timothy's command to care for widows who are without financial support (see 1 Timothy 5:1-16) a directive to take us back to the togetherness and shared life we saw in Acts 4:34 where we read, "There were no needy persons among them"? I believe so. And by doing so it again gives the potentially stark directive a human context of care, support and practical love. Much of 1 Corinthians is written to correct problems in the church. Paul writes, "some...have informed me that there are quarrels among you" (1 Corinthians1:11) and that "your meetings do more harm than good" (1 Corinthians 11:17), all of which leads him to expound at length the picture of the church as a harmoniously, united, functioning body – he takes them back to the picture (I Corinthians 12:12-27).

We could go on. Keep thinking about and exploring for yourself all that the New Testament has to say about how we should live and act as the church. It is fascinating and challenging. I believe you will find yourself coming back time and time again to the simple pictures we explored in the previous chapter and the action we examined in the early chapters of Acts, as being the nearest thing the Bible has to offer as guiding principles to build "the church everyone wants."

From the general to the specific

From those pictures and that action you now have to develop your personal ecclesiology – what you believe the church in your community should look like. It will dictate all you do: your methods, ministries, emphases, themes, events and structures.

As church-builders, our life's work is now to work with God in a process of applying the guiding principles found in the New Testament pictures of the church and its resulting action. Our task is not to build "the church *everyone* wants," but rather "the church God wants *you* to build"; the church God has spoken to *you* about, that is perfectly shaped for your community and the best possible vehicle of his life where you are building the church of Jesus Christ.

To this we now turn, from the general to the specific, from the guiding principles to their specific personal application.

Section 2:
Getting Specific

The Church God Wants You To Build

Chapter 4

The Church God Wants You To Build:

Understanding Why

What does "the church God wants *you* to build" look like? Unless you know, you are building aimlessly. As we have already established, it is insufficient to just say, "I want a church like the one in Acts," and it is certainly never possible to copy, imitate or franchise any other church model; we are in the business of building bespoke expressions of God's multifaceted community where we live.

So what is your plan? Just as every building project is constructed in accordance with a set of drawings that originated as an idea in the mind's eye of the architect, so is every successful church. Every church-builder has a picture, concept or idea of the kind of church they want to build and be a part of in their specific location.

The first question I want you to consider is, where did that idea come from? The easy answer is to say, "From God," and I hope that is the truth. But before taking that for granted it is prudent to examine more closely where your church-building blueprint actually came from. Whose idea was it? What factors brought you to your specific conclusions? It certainly came from somewhere! And the better you understand its source, the more deliberately and securely you will build.

Positive and negative drivers

In the formative days of our reinvention of the Abundant Life Church, God took us on a journey to explore our conceptual roots so that we fully understood not just what we were building but why. That included our thinking through the kind of church we did not want to build before crystallising the definite features we did want to see in the church we were about to repurpose.

Many great ministries, movements and churches emerged from a complaint! People saw a problem and decided they should do something about fixing it. William Wilberforce, for example, saw the scourge of slavery in his day and decided to fix it.

John Wesley, an Anglican priest, saw the irrelevance of the church in his day to the working class masses who would never darken the door of a church or be welcome there, and fixed it by taking the gospel out to them using "open air preaching," something his friend George Whitfield had introduced him to. The resulting revival and emergence of the Methodist church was the fruit of his life's work. His complaint became his cause; what he did not want to continue building helped him define specifically what God wanted him to build.

Likewise William Booth, the founder of the Salvation Army, was grieved that the church lacked a social gospel that reached to the poor and disenfranchised of his day. Spurred on by his complaint, he developed a vision to build a church that would take the gospel to his generation in a new and exciting way; in its day it was cutting-edge. We could go on pulling examples from church history. My point is that every church-builder has to develop their specific idea of the church they believe God wants them to build by working a process that includes identifying both positive and negative drivers. The negative drivers are what spring from your complaint: the things about the church or your church in particular that you desperately want to fix. The positive drivers are your vision of new things: the new people who will be reached, the new ministries that will be born, the new influence you will be in the community and all the new ground you envision taking for God's kingdom. Both negative and positive drivers converge to help shape your blueprint.

For us, the negative drivers involved stepping back and taking a long hard look at the state of the wider church in the UK in the late 1990s and our church in particular. We discovered we had a number of complaints of a broad-brush nature about the wider church in the UK that are detailed in Paul Scanlon's book *Crossing Over*.[1] But the most important reality check came when we assessed our own church in the light of those findings.

We had become a good, predominantly white, middle-class church, with a stable financial base, excellent building facilities and a family church ethos. Our people were committed, generous and served wholeheartedly. However, we were not a true reflection of the city we were based in, which is racially and economically diverse, and if we were really honest, we were in danger of slowly growing old together. The thought of that horrified us! It seemed to contradict the very reason any church exists. Things had to change.

The positive drivers for our emerging blueprint included exposure to other successful models of church around the world. A group of our senior leadership team went to Hillsong Church, Sydney, in 1999 for what became a landmark visit. There God spoke to us in a range of ways, both personally and through public prophecy, about our journey. It was special. Our team also developed a great relationship with Pastors Tommy and Matthew Barnett of the LA Dream Centre, USA, and a number of our staff visited to learn from them. I visited Willow Creek, Chicago, USA and managed to get behind the scenes a bit, through friends who were based there.

Pastors like Casey Treat and Kevin Gerald (USA), Ray McCauley (South Africa), Paul DeJong (New Zealand) and more than I can mention here, became not only inspirational voices to learn from, but friends who encouraged us to believe in the emerging blueprint we were crafting together.

Here in the UK we found fewer inspirational models of the kind of church we felt God was talking to us about becoming. But I must mention one man in particular, the late Wynne Lewis, founding pastor of Kensington Temple (now London City Church) and by then the superintendent of the Elim Churches. He was the only person we knew in the UK at that time who had ever built a church into the thousands, and through a God-ordained circumstance he connected with Paul Scanlon and then our wider team.

Wynne became a wonderful voice of wisdom, balance and reason at a time when we felt rather vulnerable and alone. He was a spiritual statesman and some of his legacy lives on in what we have subsequently built at Abundant Life Ministries. People and churches like these gave us hope and each became one of the positive drivers behind the blueprint we developed.

As the negative and positive drivers came together a blueprint emerged. That blueprint clarified the more we took time to understand the "why" behind the "what" we were planning to build. Why did we think Bradford needed a church like the one we were planning? Why were we so certain that certain things were non-negotiable? Why did we aspire to build in the way we were incubating?

All were important questions, which you must be able to answer in your own setting. For us the result of our labours looked like:

- a new clearly-articulated *vision*
- a clear *mission* strategy to help us fulfil that vision
- the establishment of clear core values that would come to define our church *culture*

- a revised organisational *structure* to be an appropriate vehicle for the new vision, mission and culture

But most importantly on reflection, we knew where it had come from. A clear process had been worked that helped us understood the "why" behind what we were embarking on building.

These four things – vision, mission, culture and structure – will be under constant review as a church grows and evolves through its many stages of development. Each is shaped by the positive and negative drivers mentioned above and will be explored fully in due course. But first let's dig a little deeper to bottom this out thoroughly, then you will fully understand why you want to build "the church God wants you to build."

Clarifying convictions

Your convictions shape your vision, mission, culture and structure as a church. Convictions are strong motivating forces, the wellsprings of every achievement in life. What a person lives are their convictions. Sadly, many Christians never identify, develop or articulate clear convictions about anything that really matters and, consequently, live a wishy-washy nondescript life for Jesus. To build a great church you must have clear convictions.

Paul wrote to his church-building companion Timothy on this issue. He said:

"As for you, continue in what you have learned and have become convinced of, because you know those from whom you learned it, and how from infancy you have known the holy Scriptures, which are able to make you wise for salvation through faith in Christ Jesus." (2 Timothy 3:14-15)

This insightful scripture teaches us that from all that we learn in life, only some things become convictions. There is a process by which something we learn becomes an absolute conviction, a motivating force that comes to characterise our way of doing life. Central to that process is putting things to the test.

For example, imagine you have never seen a chair before. I can teach you about the engineering involved, show you calculations to prove those thin legs will hold your weight and inform you about many other people who now sit on them regularly. But it is all head knowledge, pure learning. Then one day you pluck up courage to try this chair thing out ... and it works! Before long you confidently sit down on the chair without a moment's thought and may even stand on it or pile things up on it. You now have a conviction that chairs work; they will carry your weight.

Paul is urging Timothy to "continue in" those spiritual things he has not just learned about, but tested to the point where they have become deep convictions. Those convictions would shape the church he built.

Paul also points out that Timothy's convictions have come from two distinct sources, as have ours. He is basically saying you can press on in those convictions because they come from good sources. The two sources he identifies are firstly "those from whom you learned it": in other words people like Paul – spiritual fathers, mentors, teachers and leaders. Then secondly, "the holy Scriptures": in other words, the Bible.

These same two sources have shaped every conviction you hold as a Christian and especially as a church-builder. So when you analyse the convictions that are shaping the way you build your church today, you must be clear about which source they came from. Ideally they will both be good sources, as Paul was implying to Timothy. But this may not always be the case.

The problem is that one source is potentially fallible – the people we learn from – whilst the other is infallible, the unchanging written Word of God. So, what we learn from other people must always be supported fully by the Scriptures, which are there to "make us wise."

I have to be honest with you: I once taught things to the church with apparent conviction that I now no longer believe. The convictions in question were of course supported by a certain interpretation of Scripture but the major weight behind them came from "those from whom I learned them," my spiritual mentors at the time. I was in fact teaching the "party line" and had adopted that as my conviction.

As the years went by and I looked more objectively at the Scriptures, I realised I was not teaching a personally developed conviction but one I had adopted without too much conscious effort. As a result I had to redress some things and allow my new, genuine conviction to shape the way I built the church.

This happens a lot. Christians subliminally adopt the attitudes, opinions and teachings of those they fellowship with; they are assumed to be the absolute truth and hence worthy to be the basis of a life-motivating conviction – especially when peppered with a few scriptures to support the view. It is so subtle that sometimes we cannot even identify where such opinions and convictions actually came from, they are just there somehow, by default.

So, what I am appealing for here is a willingness to analyse where each and every conviction you hold came from. Are they there by deliberate design or by default? Are they sound? Do you really believe those things or are they merely regurgitated opinions you have taken in at some point on your journey? Wherever they came from, those convictions are now shaping your church-building efforts. They are influencing the vision, mission, values, culture and structures you are including in the blueprint for your church.

Two tributaries become clear

This principle came home to me with considerable force some years ago, following a long conversation with a pastor friend.

Through it, the influence of the two tributaries that had shaped my church-building convictions became clear.

My friend and I had served together for a period in the same church context and had both been raised in the same network of churches. So we shared the same essential theology, methodologies and approach to building the local church. However, our paths separated for a few years and it was during that period I had returned to Bradford and commenced working through the fundamental reinvention of Abundant Life Church with Pastor Paul Scanlon and our team.

My friend too had moved on, successfully leading churches in different parts of the country. By the time we met again, he was very concerned about me. From where he sat it seemed I had turned my back on aspects of our shared view of the church and how it should be built today. So he was keen to explore just how and why my convictions seemed to have changed.

After catching up about our families and general progress for a while, his thoughtful enquiry arrived. It went something like: "You seem to have forsaken all we held dear about the nature of the church." My firm reply was that I had not and that I still believed as passionately as ever all I ever had believed about the nature of the church and its importance in the scheme of things. He looked unconvinced.

So now it was my turn to ask him a question. "What makes you think I have changed?" I asked. What followed were four clear observations about the way we were building the church in Bradford, which to his mind contradicted our essential, long-held view of how the church should be built. Briefly they were:

• Firstly, he said, "We have always believed the church is 'local,' yet you are allowing people from many miles away to call Abundant Life their home church. It is nonsense! How can they possibly build a biblical local church in a different city to the one they live in?"

- Secondly, "How on earth can you practically pastor and care for those people from distant towns and cities? Without a strong, cell-based church community around them they cannot possibly be adequately shepherded."

- Thirdly, "We have always believed that as local church elders we will have to 'give an account' to God for the people entrusted to our care (Hebrews 13:17). How can you possibly do that when your church is now so large that you don't even know them personally?"

- Finally, "Rather than building a 'megachurch' in one place, shouldn't you be church planting to ensure that the essence of biblical local church is appropriately small and accessible to each local community where people live?"

I thoughtfully responded to each point in turn.

- I still believe the church is "local," but who says town boundaries define what that means? Church is all about relationships, a community which gathers around a vision that resonates in the heart of each individual. If finding that requires travel, then "the church alive is worth the drive."

- I still believe completely and utterly in the need for smallness within the largeness of any church congregation. But just how that smallness is achieved does not necessarily require a formal cell-church structure. People must "devote themselves" by putting themselves into a range of smaller settings from which they will benefit.

- I still believe Hebrews 13:17 and take it very seriously as a church leader. However, I cannot be accountable for anything an individual in my care should take personal responsibility for! But I am accountable for all that I input to their lives, the advice I give, messages I preach and direction I take the church. Just what level all that happens at will depend on our mutual relationship. Some folk I know intimately but most, less well, something we understand and negotiate together. As Paul Scanlon has said, "Relationships are spatial," and especially as a leader I must know the appropriate relational space for each person I am building my church with. For many of them it is simply my responsibility to be sure that someone else is looking after them.

• Finally, I assured him I was not against a church-planting model – one where groups are broken off and planted out every time the main church reaches an unmanageable or pre-determined size – it was just not our vision, strategy or, more importantly, our skill set.

We parted as friends. But I came away acutely aware of just how much I had shifted, not in my core convictions, which were rooted in scripture and God's call on my life, but in the methodologies I had learned from those who had taught me. I was a living example of a church leader like Timothy who was revisiting his core convictions and gaining fresh clarity about the relative importance of the tributaries that had shaped both my previous and present ones.

I trust you are now beginning to understand why I am appealing for a willingness to analyse where each and every church-building conviction you hold came from. Do you really believe those things or are they merely opinions you have taken on board at some point from other respected spiritual leaders? You must check them out because wherever they came from, those convictions are now shaping the vision, mission, values, culture and structure of your church.

Church-shaping convictions

Can I therefore ask you as a fellow church-builder, to take stock of where certain key convictions came from? Stop for a moment and think through why you believe what you do about the following significant aspects of building a thriving church. By so doing, you will better understand the "why" behind the "what" you are building, and be continuing "in what you have learned and become convinced of, because you know those from whom you learned it… and the Holy Scriptures" (2 Timothy 3:14-15).

Theology

Your convictions about God shape your church-building efforts; they pervade its culture, mission, ministry expressions, pastoral system and very essence. So what do you think of God and how he should be represented to people today? What do you really believe God loves and hates? How does he view lost people, church premises and special days in the church calendar?

Is God majestic, powerful, all-knowing, all-seeing and beyond our human capacity to ever fully know? Or is God near, intimate, a friend and loving father? Or both! How does God regard people who love church, leave church, hate church or are ambivalent about church? Is God interested in politics, education, social reform, commerce or industry? Is God consistently for you, with you, watching you and interested in you? Does God require your duty, devotion, self-abasement, sacrifice, adoration, honour and love, or does he accept you unconditionally?

Whatever your answers, those beliefs all came from somewhere. That is what you need to isolate to fully understand the forces that are influencing your theology and therefore shaping the way you build God's house.

I have been fascinated to see just how our religious backgrounds and social context affect our theology once we become a Christian. For example, in countries where Roman Catholicism is the state religion and has permeated the sense of nationhood – such as Poland, Italy and some other European nations – new believers tend to still think of God in Roman Catholic terms and their whole church experience is tinged by it. Over time, re-education occurs and their theology adjusts to one closer to the biblical truth. But this pattern illustrates the importance of identifying your convictions about God, understanding where they came from and refining them consistently as your relationship and revelation of him deepens.

Be assured, your convictions about God – your essential theology – is shaping the way you do church, build church and strategise for the future of your church.

Ecclesiology

I suppose it is stating the obvious to say that your deep convictions about the church shape the way you build it. But sadly, I find many of God's people lack thought-through personal convictions about what the church should really be like. Family tradition, programmes of particular interest, the presence of the opposite sex, the opinion of a friend, even the flamboyance of the pastor – or lack of it – all influence people's attitudes to church, their church attendance, level of involvement and their deep convictions about what church should look like today.

It is vital you develop biblically sound and culturally relevant convictions about the church. Think for a moment: what do you really think of the church you are a part of and the people in it? Your contribution to its construction and development will be completely informed and directed by those thoughts. Those thoughts are your convictions even if you can't track where they came from. So as a church-builder – which is just a way of saying you want to play a full part in building the community of God's people in your location – what do you really believe about the church?

How do you believe the church should look? How should it present itself as "God's address" to the world? What form should its corporate worship, music and celebrations take? How should people dress when the church gathers? How far do you think it appropriate to use modern technologies in the church? Is the church essentially a place for Christians to gather for mutual support or a place for the unsaved to come and find Christ? What do you consider the church's place in society to be? Should the church get involved in politics, local education, or joint charitable endeavours with other community projects? Do you believe local churches should be numerically large or small ... and why do you believe that?

Like me I am sure you know people who will happily follow Christ – after all, he is irresistible – but who have firmly rejected the church. That's why these and other similar questions are vital to get you thinking about your ecclesiology. However much you may aspire to play your part in our shared task of building God's house, your involvement, enjoyment and success will ultimately be regulated solely by these personal convictions.

Giftedness

Everyone contributes to building the church through their personal gifts, skills and abilities. It is vital, therefore, that you know what yours are and have settled convictions about them.

Too many Christians are trying to be something they can never be, simply because God has not shaped them for the thing they aspire to be. Churches are rife with this problem, which only breeds counterproductive competitiveness and selfish ambition.

However much you aspire to be a worship leader, it is never going to happen if you lack musical ability. And neither is an ambition to be an Ephesians 4:11-style apostle, prophet, evangelist, pastor or teacher going to be fulfilled unless God has gifted and anointed you to be one. This applies, then, to both natural abilities and spiritual gifts. You will build most effectively when you use the ones you have, rather than ones you wish you had!

I have a deep conviction that all I can be is the best Stephen Matthew on the planet! I must excel at being me. That means gaining an understanding of how God has made me, wired me and gifted me. There is nothing better than looking in the mirror and acknowledging that I am a unique human being, crafted by God for a specific purpose, for which he has equipped me. From that secure place I can develop my passions, gifts and abilities and put them to work helping to build God's house.

It took me many years to settle some aspects of this for myself. I had to acknowledge that the church I had grown up in had subliminally shaped my expectations of what a blessed life looked like, what a church leader looked like and what a successful church-builder or worker looked like. Hence I sought to be more like some of my peers than myself, which only led to failure, pain and frustration.

On one memorable occasion I sat with Keri Jones, one of my spiritual fathers, and discussed these matters insofar as they were affecting my role in Christian ministry at the time. After much deliberation on my part, he looked me in the eye and said, "Steve, let me tell you what I believe you are." I paused and waited for the revelation. "You are a teacher, administrator, pastor," he continued, "and definitely in that order."

In that moment something settled in me for all time because he was spot-on. That is exactly what I am and as we continued chatting we found the evidence for these observations in a myriad of examples. That conversation contributed to my liberation! I was becoming me and very happy to be so.

As a result, I stopped trying to be a front-line prophetic preacher like some of my peers. I stopped trying to be the career evangelist I envied others for being. I ceased worrying that whilst I was pastorally gifted it did not completely define me; it was appropriate for me to pastor through my primary gift, which was teaching. I stopped being negative about my love of good organisation and order as being somehow less spiritual that other gifts. Peace came, and in times of peace people flourish.

I since developed a module of teaching to help people identify their spiritual shape. It was based on an acronym of the word NICHE, the idea being to help people find their niche in the life of the church. The acronym stands for:

N – Natural abilities
I – Imparted spiritual gifts
C – Character and personality
H – Heart: the things you love to do and are passionate about
E – Experiences: everything life has taught you so far

This was taught in a class, after which each individual had a personal conversation with one of the pastoral team of the church. The idea was to help people identify where they could best get involved in helping us build the church. We realised that if they did it with their latent gifts and abilities, they would be both personally fulfilled and bear more fruit. We were empowering them to soar with their strengths as fellow builders of God's house.

In his excellent book, *The Purpose Driven Church*,[4] Rick Warren presents an even better acronym based on the word SHAPE, designed to help believers understand the way God has shaped them for service. It stands for:

S – Spiritual gifts: God's power working through us in specific ways
H – Heart: the things you love to do and are passionate about
A – Abilities: your natural gifts, talents and abilities
P – Personality: your essential personality type
E – Experiences: everything life has taught you so far

I mention both to emphasis the point: unless you develop clear, accurate convictions about your giftedness and personal skill set, you will never experience the liberation of being your God-shaped self and building the church in your God-given niche!

So, what are your convictions about your personal skill set, gifts and abilities?

Personality

You will note that in Rick Warren's SHAPE acronym he lists P for personality, and though I included C for character and personality, personality is what I was really seeking to highlight.

Character is formed, it develops and changes as we grow and mature in both natural and spiritual realms. As Christians we aim to become more like Jesus and to develop his character, which is something we all can and must do. Character speaks of maturity, strength, stability, goodness, self-discipline, faithfulness, loyalty and more. Character supports our giftedness, and lack of good character is the single greatest thing that brings down gifted people prematurely.

Personality, on the other hand, is more fixed. Your personality is your essence as a person, your hard wiring, your essential constitution. Personality is unrelated to your giftedness and your character. Your gift will be expressed through your personality, whatever type you are. God designed it that way.

So for example, if you are a gifted teacher, the way you communicate will always be influenced by your personality whether you are extrovert, introvert, reflective, phlegmatic or whatever … none are better than others, they are just states of being, expressions of human personhood. So, to be truly effective and the best teacher possible, you must be yourself and express your gift through your unique personality.

There are many personality tests available today. You can surf them up online, find them in all good bookstores and will be directed by good friends to what has helped them. Many companies routinely "personality test" their employees today in an effort to get the best out of them – a good thing, in my opinion.

I have found that some tests worked extremely well for me – maybe they suited my personality! But others were less helpful. Of course, they are all only as good as the information you feed into them, so doing it with someone who knows you really well is always helpful... but it can make you cringe! A good personality test is far more comprehensive than helping you simply isolate whether you are an introvert or an extrovert; it explores your attitudes, reactions, aptitudes and decision-making processes in an effort to give you a clear idea about your essential self.

Personally, I was most helped by Marcus Buckingham's StrengthsFinder test. It is an online test, accessed by a code provided in your personal copy of his book, *Now Discover Your Strengths*.[5] It is based on a vast reservoir of statistical data and defines very carefully the difference between a skill, a talent and a strength: a strength being an essential expression of your personality. The test responses are analysed and you are provided with an indication of your top five strengths out of a possible thirty-four. Mine were so accurate it was scary!

Why bother with all this? So that you better understand your personality and develop accurate convictions about your essential self. The result will empower you to play your part in building God's house more effectively and liberate you to enjoy the process to the full.

Community

What do you believe about the community you are building your church in? By community I mean the specific village, town, city or region your church is in. What do you think of its population and their local quirks – because we all have them! What kind of people are they? What historic events have shaped their cultural mindsets? Are they relatively prosperous, poor or somewhere in between?

Is the community cosmopolitan and racially diverse, or fairly mono-cultural? Do certain religious, philosophical or historic attitudes pervade the majority of people? What kind of reputation does your community have in the wider consciousness of your country or region? All these things are shaping your personal conviction about the church community you are building there.

Over the years, many a church leader has told me about their community, "This is a hard place to build a church." They will then proceed to explain why. "The occult is strong here," I have heard many times, along with, "There are religious strongholds resisting our growth." Some say, "The people are so hard here and always resist the gospel." In contrast, others have said "The people here are so prosperous they don't think they need God."

Maybe we have all entertained such or similar thoughts when trying to rationalise why our churches were not growing as fast as we would have liked, but for the most part these are poor excuses for not building a church that is truly relevant to the needs of the surrounding community. How much better to take a step back and do some proper "market research" into the nature of the community you are reaching, and then allow your findings to inform your convictions about how you should build?

Readers familiar with Rick Warren's book *The Purpose Driven Church*[4] will recall how, on first arriving in Saddleback, he conducted research of this kind to better understand the lives of the people in the community around the church. The result was a character called "Saddleback Sam" who he describes as being "the typical unchurched man who lives in our area."

Inspired by this, I set about trying to define "Bradford Bob"! I discovered that it was not as easy as it sounds because our city is culturally, racially and socio-economically very diverse. However, by focusing our research more locally rather than thinking citywide, we were able to compile a reasonably accurate profile of the average person who lived within the immediate area surrounding our church campus. Armed with that understanding, over the years we have been able to reach into that inner-city community, relate to people with understanding, and help them at their point of need.

I have concluded that every community in the world has its mindsets, and if we are ever to build thriving churches there, we must understand and work with them. But more than that, we must love them. Christians who genuinely love their town, city or community build their churches most effectively. Of course I do not mean loving its architecture or geography, I mean its people.

If your fundamental attitude – and conviction – is that the people in your community are losers, or are marked chiefly by some other negative trait, you will find it hard to love them appropriately. The truth is, we were all losers yet God still loved us and sent Jesus to die for us so that we could be reconciled to God and become part of his family. God's grace is amazing!

It is that kind of love – the God kind – that we must have for our communities; a love that sees beyond surface attitudes and local characteristics to the yearning within every human heart to be accepted and loved, and to belong. But to do that effectively, we have to skilfully negotiate local mindsets, attitudes and traditions, which means we have to do the research and get a true understanding of the nature of our community.

Your deep convictions about the nature of your community are significantly influencing how far you are involved in building the church there and the way in which you are doing it. So, take some time to talk to God about your attitude to your community and catch his heart for those wonderful, unique people. Allow the love of Christ that has been "poured into your heart" (Romans 5:5) to shape your convictions about them and motivate you to reach them.

Congregation
Back in the early 1980s, when I first began to emerge as a leader in the church, I recall visiting churches much larger than mine and

thinking how fortunate they were to have such a large pool of people to draw on. We always seemed to be short of help, and particularly leaders. Over the years I've discovered this is a universal problem in visionary churches: we always seem to have more vision than people to make the vision a reality right now, or money to pay for it! Consequently we find ourselves thinking, "If only we had more people, or more gifted people..."

The problem with this attitude is that it focuses on what we lack, not on what we already have, and if that becomes a conviction it impedes our ability to build with the congregation we currently have. Before long we subliminally come to regard our people as a burden, the "cross we have to bear," rather than the blessing they truly are.

It therefore saddens me when I hear church members, especially leaders, moaning about the inadequacies of their congregation because they are unwittingly expressing the conviction they hold, which is very damaging in terms of shaping their church culture. If left unchanged, it becomes virtually impossible for them to build effectively together, leading only to frustration and blame-casting when things fail to happen in the way everyone had hoped.

But I love it when people speak about their church with a sparkle in their eye and genuine affection in their voice. This is "my church" they say, exuding a sense of pride. "These are great people," they eagerly tell you.

I was greatly helped in developing my conviction about the people in the church I help lead by pastor Tommy Barnett, famous for establishing the LA Dream Centre. As mentioned earlier, one of his "life messages" is explored in his book of the same title, *There's a Miracle in Your House.*[2] In it he recalls looking at his small congregation of dysfunctional people, most of whom were former drunkards, drug addicts or convicts, and wishing he had "better people" to build the church with.

God gave him a clear revelation that within those people were all the resources he needed for what God wanted him to do in the next season. All he had to do was unlock that potential and release the miracle that was already in the house. The story that followed is amazing and well worth a read.

For me, it changed forever my conviction about the people in my church: they are miracles waiting to happen. I therefore must set about helping them discover their strengths and God-given potential, and create a context within which they can release it to help us build the church. Of course, sometimes the miracle we want hasn't arrived yet! Which is another lesson we must learn: all effective church-building ministries succeed because of effective leadership.

So, no matter how much I want to have a ministry to the elderly in our community, until I have a person with a passion to make it happen all our efforts will fall short. Experience has taught me that it is better to wait for that person to arrive rather than trying to make it happen just because we reason that every great church has a significant ministry to the elderly. Everything is "beautiful in its time" (Ecclesiastes 3:11) and sometimes we just have to wait for that right time when the miracle arrives in the form of a person who becomes the catalyst for that ministry.

That was exactly what happened to me some years ago. As a leadership team we had from time to time pondered the fact that we did not have a prison ministry. Yet we are based within reasonable distance of a number of high, medium and low-security establishments. Our Community Outreach director at the time would make occasional attempts to get access to visit prisoners and to build relationships with the prison chaplains. But it always came to nothing. So, we reasoned that the miracle was not in our house yet.

Then one day a fairly new member of our church asked to see me. He was a big but soft-hearted man – the gentle giant kind!

With tears in his eyes he explained how he had previously served in prison ministry for many years. But through a set of poor choices he had subsequently fallen on bad times and ended up in prison himself. So the prison visitor became the prisoner.

Though shocking, that experience had reinforced in him the desire to reach out and help those in prison and to be there for them when they returned into the community. His large heart was broken because he now had a criminal record, which potentially prevented him ever doing such work again. But he desperately wanted to develop a team of others he could work alongside, empower and release into prison ministry.

In that conversation our prison ministry was born. Today we send teams, all initially trained and inspired by him, into all the prisons in our region and regularly see men and women come to Christ there. It's awesome! And best of all, he has now been granted security clearance to visit some institutions himself. I love it! All we had to do was wait until the miracle was in the house, then resource, empower and release it.

I do hope you love God's people, the "living stones" you are building with in your congregation. Only then will you build effectively and in the light of your true convictions. I love my church; they are the best people in the world! But I am of course totally biased, as you should be too about your congregation.

Leadership

I don't know if you are reading this book as a church leader or as a congregational team player and follower. But, this final conviction relates to you whichever you consider yourself to be right now.

Let me start with the leaders. What are your convictions about why you are in leadership?

Over the years I have met leaders who seem to be motivated by vastly contrasting convictions. Some lead because they are convinced it is their destiny, confidently declaring, "I was born to lead." Others lead simply because no one else was willing to. They are the "reluctant leaders" in God's house and there are quite a lot of them out there.

The "born leaders" typically wrestle with issues of personal pride and have to work a process with God to take their ego to the cross and leave it there. The reluctant leaders, on the other hand, typically struggle with issues of personal worth and inadequacy, which they too must take to the cross and find a place of confident peace to be themselves. Then there is every shade of leadership between these extremes.

Some are leading because they were asked to, others because they feel they ought to. Some genuinely have a latent desire to and others just can't stop themselves taking leadership of all and every situation they find themselves in.

My point is that every successful leader leads because of a deep conviction about why they are in leadership. They know why they are leading, what and who they are leading, and where they are leading people to. They also have some sense of conviction about whether their leadership is temporary or permanent, a life-long calling or a short-term, seasonal role to fill a gap or see a project through.

Then there are the levels of leadership to reckon with. Are they shaped to be a senior leader or a support team leader? Is their capacity to lead a church or team of 10, 100 or 1,000?

In addition, all they believe about the nature of leadership will permeate their efforts. Is leadership a team exercise or a hierarchy? Do leaders consult or just issue orders? Do they lead the charge from the front or from a place alongside the team? Are leaders born or made? And how is leadership defined anyway? Do they believe John Maxwell's conclusion that "leadership is influence"[6], thus making it a very broad generic dynamic open to everyone, or is leadership restricted to the specifically gifted?

All these and related questions need to be thought through and there is an abundance of resources out there to help you. So, how do you believe biblical leadership principles should be outworked in the church today? Your answers to these and other leadership-related questions are helping you articulate your personal convictions about why you are in leadership and the way you are doing it.

Please take some time to work out your core convictions about the nature of leadership in general and your personal expression of biblical leadership. Think through where those convictions came from and allow God to take you on a personal voyage of discovery to becoming the leader he has shaped you to be.

"But I am not a leader!" I hear some of you cry. And to you I would simply say, "What makes you think that?" because you also need to know where those convictions have come from. Why don't you believe you are a leader? That conviction came from somewhere: was it from others, from the scriptures, or both...or neither? If John Maxwell's definition that "leadership is influence" is correct, you lead every time you influence another person, whether it's for good or bad. Think about it.

Finally, both to leaders and those who do not classically see themselves as such right now, I would ask, "What do you think of your leaders?" Your view of those in leadership roles towards you is closely related to your ability to build God's house effectively. We will explore this further in due course, but for now I am asking you to isolate why you have the attitude towards leadership you currently hold? Where did that conviction come from? It will seriously help or hinder your ability to build the church together.

I hope I have not left you with more questions than answers! But the second part of this book is entitled *Getting Specific: The Church God Wants **You** To Build*, which is impossible to do without understanding yourself and the core convictions that are shaping the way you are building God's house.

My prayer is that as you talk with God about what you believe and why, across the whole range of issues we have touched on in this chapter, you will become secure in who you are and better understand your church-building motivations. What a person lives are their convictions, and those God-guided convictions are what will eventually get the church he wants you to build off the drawing board and into action.

But before we get really practical, there is one final exercise we need to do on the drawing board to ensure we can build with confidence.

Chapter 5

the Church God Wants You To Build:
Developing The Plan

Preparation is everything! Whether you are performing a drama, making a speech, taking an exam, redecorating a room, taking a year out, building a house, landscaping your garden, starting a new job or building the church, the final result will be directly linked to your preparation. It is a fact of life.

However, we tend to equate preparation with new starts, and when it comes to building the church we rarely get to start the whole process from scratch. Most of us are not church planters or in a position of taking on an existing church and shaping its whole redevelopment. Consequently, we concentrate on the smaller new starts that feature in church life and we plan diligently for those. We may start a new outreach programme, a new training event or ministry initiative, and that initiative gets our full attention as we prepare thoroughly for its launch.

But do we ever take a step back and re-think the whole way we are building our church? If we don't, there is a danger that each new initiative gets bolted on to the last one without an overarching sense of strategic planning.

How, for example, do each of the initiatives launched over the last few years interface with each other? Do they compete for resources? Is their focus dominating the direction of the church or just one expression of it? Is that ministry still really needed? Left unchecked, over the longer term church can easily become a jumble, a random collection of ministry initiatives with no central cohesion or reason for being that is consciously anchored in the present vision of the church.

Because this is the nature of building the church, we need to become adept at not only planning and launching specific projects, but also at doing so within the larger framework of our overall building plan. This, of course, demands that such a plan exists, and I have been surprised by just how many churches do not have one – or at least one that is easily articulated.

Developing a clear, God-guided plan as a basis for your church-building efforts is crucial. On reflection this was one of the biggest lessons I learned through the process of reassessing how we wanted to rebuild the Abundant Life Church back in the late 1990s. It left me acutely aware that any church-building or rebuilding process is shaped by four fundamental things, which together make up the overall development plan for building God's house in any community. Those four things are: vision, mission, culture and structure.

These are buzzwords in church-building circles. We use them frequently, assuming everyone knows what we mean. But if we are to be serious and effective church-builders they must become words that carry precious revelation, truth and strategy about the way we are specifically building God's house in our location. They are building blocks – potentially the four cornerstones of your church building, and if any one of them is weak or flawed, your building will become unstable. That's how important they are.

Vision

Vision is all about what you see. Vision is what you envisage, what you see in your mind's eye. Your vision is like the artist's impression of a new building that is still on the drawing board – even though it is not yet fully built, you see it and are determined to see that vision become a reality. Vision is what you are aiming for, building towards, the consummation of your efforts.

Vision gives definition to the way you are building your church; it explains why you do certain things in certain ways. It positively constrains all you do within clearly stated parameters that will inevitably result in the vision becoming a reality. As Proverbs 29:18 says, "Where there is no vision the people cast off restraint."

Your church vision is that positive restraint. It stops people doing random things that are unrelated to, or damaging to, the church God has called you to build. Vision galvanises everyone around a common desire to make the vision a reality. But without a God-given vision of the kind of church you are building in your community, people simply "stumble over themselves" (Proverbs 29:18, The Message).

It is for these reasons I always try and find out the vision of any church I am visiting. If I am going to help them build I need to know their vision, otherwise my contribution may detract from their building efforts. I want to know what they are building towards, what inspires them and unites them as a congregation to work together in the way they are.

When we spent time reinventing the Abundant Life Church back in the late 1990s, we soon realised that until we had the vision agreed, everything else we tackled had no context, no end game. Everything had to contribute towards the fulfilling of a vision, so we had to start there. And it took a considerable time to get it right.

We had to think through every aspect of the church we wanted to build and get to the essence of what God was speaking to us about. Developing a vision to build towards takes prayer, research, discussion and many failed attempts to articulate. But eventually you will get it so right that every time you read those words your heart will warm and your spirit leap, and in your heart you will be saying "Yes! That's the kind of church I want to be a part of!"

I can honestly say that every time I read our vision statement, it moves me. It never gets old or tired. I am reminded of how wonderful it is to be in a church like this and am also provoked to work hard to ensure we continue building true to that vision. I know this because every year in our Leadership Academy we do an exercise where we break the vision statement down into its constituent phrases and ask a student to speak about each phrase in turn, giving biblical and anecdotal evidence for its appropriateness in building a great church. And it always moves me!

In addition, every year as a church we give a Vision Offering, a special one-off offering towards the accomplishment of the vision. Inevitably we restate the vision, the same vision we have been proclaiming for over twelve years now, and it remains fresh as the day it was drafted. The vision does not need to change until it is fully built, and if it takes a lifetime, so be it.

Here are the words I am referring to. Each one is pregnant with truth, purpose and revelation, an indispensable building block to inform the way we are building God's house in our community. Because vision is all about what we see in the future, we call it "The church I see":

The church I see...

The church I see is God-centred, purpose-driven and people-empowering.

The church I see is exciting and full of life. It is a church that is both numerically large and spiritually deep.

The church I see is non-religious, naturally supernatural, and incredible fun to be in. It's a church of renowned character and integrity, a church whose number one priority is to glorify God and bring his wonderful life to a lost world.

The church I see is attractive, confident, victorious and overcoming. I see a church whose powerful proclamation and awesome worship are broadcast to the nations by every modern means possible.

The church I see equips, enables and releases ordinary people to live extraordinary lives.

The church I see is a deeply committed, loving, caring family amongst whom the lonely and the broken find refuge, new hope and belonging.

The church I see could well be this church, the Abundant Life Church, Bradford.

Having read vision statements from churches around the world I am aware that many are similar to this. That's to be expected, because we are all unique local expressions of the one universal church in the world. Some are shorter, others longer, but every one is a fascinating insight into the church leaders who crafted that particular form of words, then cast that vision for people to gather around.

What ultimately matters is that each individual person – each "living stone" in your building – genuinely owns those words. That's why we went for "the church I see" rather than "the church we see." It takes a personal agreement for each person to live, act, speak and build towards making that vision a reality. Only then does it become "the church we see."

This came home to me strongly at one of the Leadership Academy exercises I described above. The students had each drawn by lot an aspect of the vision statement they would speak on. One of the final phrases was expounded by Bimala, a delightful student from Nepal. She made the simple but profound point that the church is people, "living stones," which included her.

So she said that the way the statement should actually read was "the Bimala I see is …" On she went, "the Bimala I see is…God-centred…attractive…naturally supernatural…overcoming…a loving caring family." Oh my! Talk about driving the thought home; there were quite a few tears in the room that day.

When vision is truly caught in your spirit, it moves you! Ever since that day I have encouraged people to read our vision statement and insert their name. "The church I see" is first the church I agree to be! Only then will it become a reality. I must first commit to becoming those words and only then will we collectively fulfil that vision.

In his book *IT*, subtitled *How churches and leaders can get it and keep it*[7], Craig Groeschel makes a convincing case for vision being an indispensable ingredient of all churches that have "it." He says, "Ministries that have it always have clear vision. The people know the vision, understand the vision, believe in the vision and live the vision. The vision guides them, motivates them and energises them. Large numbers of people move in the same direction. Churches with vision tend to have *it*. All the rest are hit and miss."

However long it takes, get your vision statement right. It is not a random collection of Christian buzzwords; it is the essence of who you are and what you are building together. It is a cornerstone of your building. "Where there is no vision, the people perish" (Proverbs 29:18 KJV) – it is that important!

Mission

The second cornerstone to articulate clearly as part of the church-building process is your mission.

I find many people mix up mission and vision. Sometimes they are merged together as a single statement but this can be confusing to analytical church-builders like me! So forgive me if you think I am splitting hairs on this one – I assure you I am not. Mission is very different from vision.

The vision is the end product, where we are going and what we are becoming. The mission is what we do to get ourselves there. The vision is the destination, and the mission is the vehicle that takes us to it. Your mission statement basically says, "If we do these things, we believe we will build a church that looks like our vision."

So, what are the features that constitute our mission? Of all the four cornerstone-like foundations on which you are building your church, this is the one we share completely in common. Even though we live in different parts of the world with their diverse cultures and in communities with very distinct characteristics that certainly influence our methodologies, our mission is the same:

"Go and make disciples of all nations, baptizing them in the name of the Father and of the Son and of the Holy Spirit, and teaching them to obey everything I have commanded you." (Matthew 28:19-20)

This is what Jesus commanded us to do; it is our mission. Jesus spoke similar words to the apostle Paul at the point of his salvation:

"I am sending you ... to open their eyes and turn them from darkness to light, and from the power of Satan to God, so that they may receive forgiveness of sins and a place among those who are sanctified by faith in me." (Acts 26:17-18)

Jesus himself had a mission. He came to do something very specific and now we – those who are "in Christ" – have become the enduring expression of that mission in the world today. Jesus said:

"The Spirit of the Lord is on me, because he has anointed me to preach good news to the poor. He has sent me to proclaim freedom for the prisoners and recovery of sight for the blind, to release the oppressed, to proclaim the year of the Lord's favour." (Luke 4:18-19)

And that is now what we do; it is our mission. It is what the church exists for, its reason for being, it is our primary purpose. A good mission statement gathers up this great commission that we all share and articulates it in a way that has specific meaning and practical expression for its particular congregation. Some are very long statements describing specific mission strategies and initiatives that gather up every participating member of the church, while others are short and succinct, leaving the detail to other contexts. There is no right or wrong! You just need one.

Because the church is a living, growing organism, it will be forever changing and outworking the mission in creative ways as its composition changes. I therefore think the best mission statements are *short* enough to be memorable, *local* enough to be "yours" and *long* enough to accommodate every expression of the Great Commission. That might seem a tall order! But it is achievable if you take the time to prayerfully develop it as a leadership team and not just grab one off the shelf of another church you admire.

This is how it went for us. I don't include this because I regard it as being the ultimate mission statement – it is just the best way to illustrate my point.

As we progressively reinvented the Abundant Life Church, the words of our vision and mission statements began to clarify. For us it was vital that we made one phrase top of the list when it came to the mission statement, mainly because it had been too far down the list for many of the previous years and we wanted to make a strong statement of intent. That phrase was "Reach the lost." So that's where we started and the rest evolved from there.

As we thoughtfully applied ourselves to finding phrases that would express the essential mission of the church but in our context, God led us to a particular verse: Revelation 11:1, where the apostle John says, "I was given a reed like a measuring rod and was told, 'Go and measure the temple of God and the altar, and count the worshippers there.'"

A number of things struck us about this verse, not least that the measuring rod was a reed. In ancient times reeds from the riverbank were used as measuring rods because unlike metal and wood they did not expand or contract as weather conditions changed. The reed was a consistent measure. And we needed to have a consistent measure of what we considered to be the mission through which we built our "temple," God's house, the church.

Eventually an acronym developed based on the word reed, the four phrases of which have become our mission statement. These four things have become the headings under which we do all we do. If something does not fit into one of them, we do not do it because it is not part of our mission. It's that clear. The acronym is:

Reach the lost
Establish the church
Equip the saints
Disciple the nations

This not only maintained "reaching the lost" as our primary mission objective but gave some sense of process to the discipleship, empowering and releasing process that comes next. This is our cycle of life! We reach the lost, establish those lost people in a thriving church community, equip them with the tools to live a successful Christian life and then release them to go and make more disciples from every nation possible. In principle it is the same outreach and discipleship cycle that every church follows, just expressed in a way that made it personal to our church. So what we adopted as our mission statement is *short* enough to be memorable, *long* enough to embrace all aspects of our mission, and *local* enough to be ours.

Each of these phrases is pregnant with meaning for me – much like the vision statement. They are not Christian clichés but vehicles of our essential mission. For example, as a pastor my intention is to "reach the lost" within every person in our church.

Reaching the lost is not just about saving souls, that's only the starting point! Once saved, there are dreams, gifts, abilities, passions and aspirations for us to seek out and release in every unique individual. And it can take years before all the "lostness" is found. So as I preach, counsel and support people in their Christian journey, I am assisting them on a path to discover all that God made them to be but was buried under the debris of sin and a life lived outside of Christ. I love it!

To effectively play your part in building your local church, whether it is as a leader or team member, you must have a felt sense of outworking the mission. It must become personal.

I remember as a teenager going on summer missions with Don Hinchcliffe, a well-known evangelist in the Brethren circles I grew up in, a wonderful man of God. Don took groups of us on beach missions and we did village evangelism in the Yorkshire Dales. I vividly remember it being drummed into me that we were outworking the Great Commission and we could all faithfully quote Matthew 28:19-20. Yet if I am honest, I never really connected with the text. I understood it was our essential mission but it lacked the personal ownership required for it to become a life-propelling conviction.

And I think many Christians are like that. They know we are supposed to be mission-minded and can quote the key texts, but they don't feel anything and hence remain unmoved and inactive.

At worst, in obedience to Paul's exhortation to Timothy they "do the work of an evangelist" (2 Timothy 4:5) but with a bad attitude! This damages both them and the people they are trying to reach.

So my appeal to you as someone who wants to build a thriving church in your community – which is why I assume you are reading this book – is that you take the time to fully engage with the mission statement of your church. If needed, rewrite it and re-express it.

Talk with God about how to creatively express your mission in a way that makes it accessible and relevant to every person in your congregation. Make it as long or short as you like, but do give it a local flavour. Then take personal ownership of it. Get it into your head and heart; speak it, write it, sing it and most of all live it!

Culture

Of the four cornerstone-like features that underpin your church-building efforts, we now come to the most difficult to articulate: the culture.

Every church has a distinct culture. It is just there, permeating all that is said and done. It is in the atmosphere people walk into and resides in the established mindsets that tend to govern people's attitudes and responses. It is the thing that visitors take away with them, whatever has been said to the contrary.

For example, no church would claim to be unfriendly. They might point to their car park attendants, ushers on the door to welcome people, stewards to guide people to their seats, a statement of welcome in the church bulletin and a welcome announcement from the front each week as proof of their intent to be friendly.

But this is pure structure, not culture. To have a friendly, welcoming culture, everyone has to be friendly, from top to bottom. Not just those with the appropriate badges, but every person in every seat who the visitor may end up sitting next to.

As Kevin Gerald points out in his insightful book on this subject, every church has a culture either by *Design or Default.*[8] Our task as church builders is to make sure it is the former. We must deliberately craft the culture of our church by establishing very clear values that we want to characterize our church.

This is very important because everything we do is communicated and mediated through our culture. For example, our culture is present in the way we package and present the gospel, which is a massive responsibility. Jesus is irresistible, but the church is sometimes very resistible, in fact it can put people off Christianity altogether. That is fundamentally a cultural issue.

Similarly, your church culture determines who attends. Some church cultures are attractive to men, others repel them. Some attract families, or young people, or the socially disadvantaged. When a leader looks across a church and asks himself, "Why don't we have any business people in our congregation?" there is potentially a cultural issue involved.

When we were reinventing the Abundant Life Church, we observed that we had very few non-white people in our congregation and very few poor people. Both were linked to cultural mindsets that were present but which we never remember putting in place. They were there by default not design. So we made a decision to completely redesign the culture.

Crafting the new vision statement and mission strategy was easy when compared to changing the culture of the church. Because culture is so pervasive, it affects everybody whether they like it or not. It is culture change that causes people to leave a church, not a re-drafted vision or mission statement. But equally, it is culture change that attracts new people to you! That is why it has to be right.

We spent time analyzing our existing church culture, putting words to it and isolating the aspects we disliked. In their place we established new words that described the culture we wanted to characterize our new church. The full process is explored in *Crossing Over* by Paul Scanlon. In addition I highly recommend you read

Pastor Kevin Gerald's book *Design or Default*, if you are currently in a process like this. The words we chose to define our culture were ones like these:

God-centred – By that we meant our church would not be people-centred, issue-centred, money-centred, gifted leader-centred, denomination-centred, pet theology-centred, but centre only around God. We would frequently state that "It is all about Jesus" and nobody else – and mean it! And our consequent actions and lifestyle would be the proof.

Purpose-driven – By that we meant two things. First, that everything we did would be inherently purposeful. So any and every meeting or ministry activity that was essentially purposeless would be scrapped. And second, we were saying we intended to do all we did in line with God's higher purpose. It was not our purpose but God's that mattered.

People-empowering – By this we were stating one of the most fundamental changes we made to our culture. We would be people-empowering not people-controlling. We would make it our aim to help people locate their talents, strengths, abilities and passions and then empower them to use them as an expression of our church life and ministry. We would take risks with people, empower the young, stand by them when they failed and gain a reputation for being "second chance central," as a local newspaper report once described us.

Paul Scanlon subsequently described these three things as being "jewels lost from the church's crown" and they have consequently become our primary core values as a church. They have shaped and informed all we do over time – and it does take time to change the culture of a church in this way.

We preached message after message to help people catch the spirit of the new church culture we were crafting together, and then started to make changes in light of those emphases. We had to deal with the discomfort this caused as longstanding members gradually realized we were serious about changing things. Some left, unable to embrace the emerging culture. But others came and thrived in the freedom of the empowering church culture we were developing.

Beyond these three values, a number of other words become very important culture descriptors to us over time. Words like:

Devotion – A very early and consistent theme in our reshaping of the church culture was rooted in Acts 2:42 where it says of the people who came to Christ after Peter's sermon at Pentecost, "They devoted themselves to the apostles' teaching, the fellowship, the breaking of bread and to prayer." This devotion has become a major feature of our church culture.

We expect people to devote themselves to Jesus, to reading his word, to prayer and being together. Without that devotion flowing from the heart of the Christ-follower, leaders spend inordinate amounts of their time coercing reluctant people to do all those things and more. We had done it for years and spotted it was a negative aspect of our old church culture that had evolved by default and we were determined to design it out.

Jesus said to his disciples, "Follow me," and kept moving; they had to take some initiative to follow him and that is what we teach our people to do. Our pastoral structures exist to support them but we will always require people to have an attitude of personal devotion to follow Christ. This has emancipated our leaders and they have been able to thrive as they now can concentrate on steering and facilitating the gift of everyone's devotion to Christ.

Inclusive – We made deliberate efforts to be all-inclusive. It is frequently made clear that we do not care where people have come from, what kind of background, lifestyle, socio-economic group, education or race. All are welcome and will be treated equally in a non-judgmental environment centred around their finding a new start in Christ.

Excellence – Ashamed that so much of the church at large was characterized by a poverty mentality which legitimized putting up with all kinds of shoddy attitudes, buildings and practices, we determined to do everything we did as excellently as possible within sensible tolerances. Excellence is not about opulence or extravagance. It is about doing the best you can with what you have and is in fact an attitude, not a material thing. We aspired to have a reputation for going the extra mile, being generous and helping the people others wouldn't touch. We aimed to do the work of the ministry every church is called to do, but with excellence.

Generational – Disturbed by the fact that a disproportionately large part of the church in the UK seemed to be led by old people, we made a commitment to empower and release the young to play their part in building God's house alongside us, as we grew older. The youth bring vitality, zeal and dynamism to any church. But those wonderful qualities need the steady, guiding and releasing hands of mature believers to steer them forwards.

So, the best thing is to develop a truly cross-generational church; one where we all play our part, from the youngest to the oldest, in an atmosphere of mutual love and support. This desire is best summed up by the words Paul Scanlon wrote about empowering our youth: "I refuse to get in their way...we are running together and will for years to come...They will go further, deeper and wider than me...God, help me to help them live their dreams. May I never be a hindrance to their progress; may I grow old watching my children and theirs shaking the planet for you. Amen!"[1] I hope you are beginning to understand just how important it is that you take control of the culture of your church, ministry team, family or business – because this principle applies across the board where people work together in a corporate environment.

The ongoing challenge is to keep it under constant review once established, because the culture of every church is constantly evolving. It evolves as existing members grow and change, as new people join, as we focus on different theological emphases, as specific ministry initiatives thrive or fail, as leaders come and go, as society changes and economic trends impact people's lives. As Kevin Gerald says: "It's not easy to constantly adjust to an evolving culture, but it is essential if a church is to remain relevant to every generation."[8]

Structure

The final cornerstone-like feature to have a thorough grasp of as you develop a plan to build or rebuild your church, is its structure. I see it this way:

- Our *vision* is what we see.
- Our *mission* is what we do to accomplish that vision.
- Our *culture* is the all-pervading manner in which we do it: our ethos, core values and way of doing things.
- Our *structure* is the organizational wrapper that holds it all together.

A church's structure must never be allowed to be more important than its culture. A good structure always facilitates the culture rather than restricting it. Sadly many church structures – the organisational skeleton from which everything hangs – have become sacrosanct over the years. The one thing you cannot change is the structure!

"We have always done it this way" is the cry of those devoted to the structure rather than the life it is supposed to be facilitating.

Stories abound of people leaving churches because the pipe organ was removed, the pews were replaced with folding chairs or the overhead projector was abandoned for a laptop computer. Even more prevalent is people's human attachment to structural systems like the board of elders, the diaconate, the one-member one-vote congregational system of church government or the way we have always organised our children's ministry. Structure has its place but must be kept in its place!

We noted earlier that the culture of a church is constantly evolving and therefore under constant review. This inevitably means, therefore, that the structure of the church has to evolve with it. Structures need to be flexible like a good wineskin, not written in stone like the infamous laws of the Medes and Persians, which could not be altered.

I recall that some time into our "crossing over" journey of reinventing the Abundant Life Church, we had grown our Kids Church significantly by bussing in families and children from local housing estates. We were being inclusive and deliberately reaching into some economically poor areas of our city. The new culture was doing its thing!

But the structure started to creak. These rather unruly children were not easily handled in the small class groups we structured our Kids Church around. To them it was too much like school and they hated school! So after researching what other churches did in similar environments we decided to change the structure and base most of the programme around larger group activities where the mischievous kids could be absorbed by the crowd and not dominate.

We introduced separate worship for them, their own band, lots of short, sharp, high-impact segments to keep them engaged and learning – and it worked. But some parents withdrew their children from the Kids Church programme and subsequently left the church because of the change. They felt their children had lost the intimacy they previously enjoyed and disliked the influx of unchurched children.

The discussions with those parents became all about the clash between culture and structure. And though it was relationally difficult, culture had to prevail. No structural element had to be allowed to stand in the way of the new wine of our emerging culture. It took courageous leadership and resolve to drive some of those structural changes through, but the vast majority of people understood, rejoiced in them and enjoyed the fruit of the changes they brought.

Structures also need to remain flexible to ensure they remain appropriate to the fluctuating seasons of church life. If they don't, they will just get in the way of what God wants done in a particular season.

For 25 years we had been a cell church structured around a system of home groups. Membership of a group was mandatory; it was impossible to be a part of our church without being in one. Everything was run through the home groups; it was how we monitored your progress, fed information to you, and ensured you were supported and discipled. We were a classic house church of the vintage that emerged in the years following the charismatic renewal of the late 1970s.

When first conceived and established, those home groups were the lifeblood of our church. Indeed, I have many fond memories of them over a period of many years. But as we navigated our reinvention of the church some 25 years later, it became clear to us they were a structural hindrance to the emerging culture rather than facilitating it.

However we still had a conviction that in a growing church everyone needs to find their smallness in the largeness; we need intimacy, smaller support groups, circles of close relationships and so on. So, our challenge became, "How do we retain an expression of that conviction about small groups, while dismantling the old structure?"

The result was a presentation I made to the church one Sunday morning in which we announced that the home groups in their existing form were to be closed – and everyone cheered, so we knew we were on track! In their place we created three kinds of alternative small groups, one based on discipleship, one based on ministry interests and one based on life-stages. People could attend one of each if they had the time or none at all.

The "three-line whip" was removed and people were released to devote themselves to these aspects of the church as they wished. The structural change was embraced by the vast majority simply because it was explained in the context of our evolving culture which they were really starting to understand and engage with. And for some of them that meant not attending a formal small group at all – which would have been anathema under the old structure.

Within a year God spoke to us about gathering the church together for a midweek service for a period and Wednesday night church was born. Many of the new small groups decided to attend that instead of meeting separately, so once again a structural change facilitated a further evolution of the culture. That change meant a significant proportion of our church were now not attached to any formal small group at all.

Eventually we ceased Wednesday night church and just let people find their fit relationally – to devote themselves for a season. And it was fine because it was a structure appropriate to the season we were in. But I do remember talking to other pastors in that period and them being horrified that we did not have a small group structure in place. So I had to keep reminding myself and the observers of our progress that the structure will always serve the culture and not the other way round.

Just in case you are now worried about us, we reintroduced a new style of small groups about two years later. We call them Life Groups and they form a key role in facilitating the life and culture of our church today.

One final example. As the Abundant Life Church has grown, our leadership structure has changed beyond recognition. I guess it is logical but the leadership structure required to run a church of 400 looks very different to the structure required to run a church of 2,000. Those changes have sometimes been difficult to navigate because individuals were reluctant to adjust personally, be line-managed in a new way, give up or take on responsibilities, have their job description or volunteer brief changed, and so on.

Another factor is the growth of the individual leaders themselves. As they make the transition into new roles and responsibilities, remaining faithful to God's call on their lives, there is a ripple effect that impacts on all those leading around them, especially when they are a high-profile leader.

So, my point is that as long as you are committed to a process of cultural change which has as its goal the accomplishment of your vision, your structures will have to remain flexible and always appropriate to the season you are in. The vision may remain the same and the mission to realise it be fundamentally fixed, but your church culture and structure will be forever changing for the better. As a committed church-builder you must never resist that change but determine to steer it positively, ensuring these cornerstone-like elements stay in place and intact until the building is done.

Chapter 6

The Church God Wants You To Build:

Let The Building Begin!

It is a truism that "preparation is everything," but eventually you have to get on with the actual building process. The church you want to build must get off the drawing board and become a physical reality. Vision must find form. Real people, "living stones," must be built together into a spiritual house in which God is pleased to dwell.

For many reading this, that will mean refurbishment, restoration or repair of an existing church community and brings with it a whole set of relational challenges to grapple with.

For others, it will be a brand-new start. I think those fortunate enough to be able to build from scratch have a great advantage as they can build in line with their vision and mission, establish their desired culture from the start and develop a flexible structure from the word go. But whichever situation you find yourself in as a church builder, I believe the steps apply equally. One of the things I like to explore with people who share my love for building thriving churches is the speed at which they think things can be accomplished. It seems some new churches grow fast and others very slowly. Similarly, some church reinventions are done in a relatively short time and others drag on for years. The factors are myriad and must be explored in their unique local context, but I have observed that to build or rebuild God's house effectively, one important thing must be understood: building a great church is not a linear exercise, it is a cyclical one.

The church-building cycle

Many a church-building attempt has failed because its leaders treated building God's house as a linear exercise. In other words, they thought that if they did a thing once or twice and got it established they could then leave it alone and move on to the next phase of the building. It would be like joining the dots in a straight line, the final dot being the realization of their vision – that awesome church of their dreams. If only ...!

Perhaps few would say they really believe church building is accomplished that way. But actions speak louder than words, and the fact is that too many church-builders end up disappointed because, despite their protestations, this was the way they built. Their tendency was to make each stage in the building process an event, a milestone, a lasting achievement.

But in reality, little remains stationary in the church-building process. All the elements have to be established, developed and maintained at the same time – which sounds like spinning a lot of plates! And it is. The key is not to be spinning them all yourself.

I prefer to describe the church-building process as a cycle. A cycle allows periodic revisiting of all the significant elements of your church-building, ensuring they remain fresh, interconnected and vibrant contributors to the overall scheme of things.

A pastor friend once bemoaned to me that his people were "doing his head in." Why? I enquired. "They just don't get what we are trying to do," he said, exasperated. By that he meant they were slow in adopting his leadership team's major redirection of the church. The church was at the front end of what I instinctively call a "crossing over." They were repurposing, re-envisioning, re-culturing and restructuring the church. It was major!

He had been the pastor for over twenty years but during the last three had increasingly felt the need to change things, and had worked a very comprehensive process with his close leadership team. To all intents and purposes he had done much of what has just been described. He knew why he was doing it – his convictions had been revisited and were intact with clear new adjustments in place.

They had developed a clear vision and mission statement, identified the kind of church they believed God wanted them to become, and begun to make some structural changes towards that end. But he felt cautiously accepted by some, resisted by others and completely misunderstood by a significant proportion of his church. He felt as if the jury was out on him and a verdict wasn't coming soon! The combined effect was slow progress that deeply frustrated him.

I assured him that I had seen it all before, which was both disappointing and reassuring at the same time. He and his close team had worked a comprehensive process that had taken them the best part of three years. They had then launched the results onto the wider church without taking into account that some of them may also need three years to process it all!

The answer was to work the "church-building cycle" and not become frustrated because some people don't catch on straight away. Indeed, expecting that to happen is really requiring everyone to build in a linear fashion. This is the vision, tick the box and move on. This is the new culture, tick the box and move on. This is our new structure, tick the box and move on ... and be quick about it please! It is "linear thinking" which will always end in disappointment in the realm of building God's house.

What then is the church-building cycle? It is a series of eight things we do to ensure that the church is built from stage to stage in a stable and cohesive manner. Here, then, are the eight things I have observed constitute the church-building cycle:

1. Communicate clear vision consistently

It all starts with communicating the vision. The church you and your leadership team have heard from God about has to be described and defined in inspiring yet accessible ways. That wonderful church of your dreams, which will become a beacon of hope in your community and a thriving expression of God's kingdom, must be articulated with clarity. Preach it clearly, teach it thoroughly, and unpack it element by element.

Let it never be said of you that the vision was "woolly" or vague in its communication. Encourage your worship team to write or find songs expressing truths from it, your kids' workers to break it down for the little ones, the youth leaders to develop a cool, street-speak version of it, and your prayer teams to pray into it. Print it on your literature, decorate your walls with phrases from it, and give everyone a fridge magnet with it on! Just do whatever you can to creatively and clearly communicate the vision.

This can take a while the first time you do it. I hesitate to put a time on it, but in our experience at Abundant Life Church it certainly took a couple of years to permeate the whole church. But what is more important to grasp is that this clear vision-casting process never ends! If it does, your momentum slows down and will eventually stop.

At least once every year the vision should be revisited and celebrated. The process gathers up new people and refreshes the existing ones. Many churches today hold Vision Sundays, an annual event where the vision is spoken about, communicated clearly and people are invited to contribute towards its accomplishment. That contribution may be financial or practical, or both.

We have successfully used the annual Vision Sunday idea to receive a significant annual Vision Offering from our people and also treated such days as a form of Ministry Fair. On those occasions we have stands with representatives from all the key areas of church for people to visit and where they can sign up to play their part in outworking this great vision. It creates a great buzz about the vision and all we are doing together.

I would also recommend regular vision-casting by church departments. As a worship, youth, children, community outreach or discipleship department, hold a regular Vision Night. Talk to your team about how your ministry area helps to accomplish the overall vision. It keeps everyone aware of the big picture and feeling a vital part of the church. If these are placed at strategic times in your church calendar, it means people cannot be in your church for long without someone inspiring them to play their part in making the vision a reality.

When it comes to communicating the vision, the key words are "clarity" and "consistency." Work hard to ensure both are in place.

2. Begin to make changes

Implementing the vision inevitably means things will have to change. Nervous church-builders will want to keep communicating the vision until they perceive everyone is on board and then start to make the changes. Consequently change will be at best slow and more likely never happen. You must commit to making changes very early in the process. Starting to make changes shows the church you are serious; the vision you have cast is not just a nice sentiment but is destined to become a tangible reality.

Knowing just where to make your first change is for you to decide. It could be anything. But it is making actual change that lights the blue touch-paper of the vision! Some will never believe you until they see this actual evidence that you mean business.

What come next is instructive. Some may leave because of it, others will be energised and rush to your side in support. The doubters will slowly become believers and the ones who have been waiting for you to "pull your finger out" will become the most committed activists.

One of the first things we did at Abundant Life Church to demonstrate that we were serious about implementing the vision we had cast, was to move the church elders off the platform. It may sound crazy to many reading this, but for the first 17 years of my life in ministry I had never sat next to my wife Kay in a church meeting. The reason was because we had a tradition of the church elders sitting on the platform behind whoever was speaking or leading.

I won't go into the historic reasons for this here but suffice to say that it had become dated and inappropriate. For most observers it simply communicated that the leadership was male and that it was watching you! If the elders smiled, the people felt secure. If the elders looked unhappy or nervous about a contribution, the people became so. It was just too "government heavy," and certainly not a reflection of the new church we aspired to build. If "the church I see" was to be both fun and attractive, it needed to pay attention to what was holding centre stage at all its events. So, one Sunday people arrived and were surprised to find us sitting on the front row next to our wives. Most smiled and thought it was a great change; a few furrowed their brows in the realisation that we were actually going through with what we had said.

Soon after that we removed the microphone for spontaneous contributions to the meeting. This was a bigger deal for some. We believed in the operation of the gifts of the Holy Spirit, and still do, but over the years we had developed a culture that restricted their use to the Sunday services. So aspiring prophets and those with a tongue to be interpreted saw it as their primary opportunity to minister to the church. They would come to the front during the worship, grab the microphone and bring their contribution in the next available gap in the flow of worship.

But one week they arrived and the microphone was gone! We had of course explained it was going to disappear and the good reasons why, but some still accused us of "quenching the Spirit." Our reasons were all connected to the vision, the church we were becoming, its accessibility for the guest and the appropriate control of elements in what was our shop window to the world. There were other smaller settings where the gifts could be expressed, but randomly on a Sunday morning was no longer one of them. Some left but again, most rejoiced and rallied around the emerging culture we were starting to model.

As I mentioned previously, the primary element of our new mission was to "reach the lost." So how better to show we were serious in our intent, than to actually start doing it in new and exciting ways? For this reason we started a bus ministry aimed primarily at bringing children and families to church from some of the more deprived parts of our city. It was a massive project. We had street teams working on the estates, building relationships with the families. These teams then fed the contacts through to the bus team who collected them and cared for them en route. On arrival at church the host team took over, ensuring they had a great experience on our campus. Their behaviour made fresh demands on our Kids Church team who needed new training to cope with them. We invested in some of our team and sent them to the LA Dream Centre to visit the bus ministry operating there.

It was like dropping a stone in a millpond! The ripples of this change affected everyone. Some left, but yet again, the majority rejoiced and poured their love, grace, time and energy into making the initiative truly life-changing. If anyone still doubted we were serious about building "the church I see," by this time they were well on their way to becoming believers.

So, making changes in line with the vision that has been clearly communicated shows you are serious as a leadership team and will begin to sift out those who really "get" what you are trying to build and those who don't.

Before moving on, let me return to the matter of how fast one can reasonably expect it to take to reinvent or repurpose an existing church, as we did at Abundant Life. As I said, we spent a good two years casting the vision, while starting to make changes, before it was widely held as normative by the church. After comparing notes with other pastors who have completed or are currently in a similar process of "crossing their church over," I have concluded that the rate of change is linked to two factors: how well the vision is communicated, and how fast you are willing to make changes.

Some communicate the vision in an apologetic manner in an effort to gather everyone up. That same disposition in a leader will also lead to reticence in making large changes until a majority are on board, both of which slow things down. Of course it takes great skill and wisdom to steer your individual course. There is no road map for this; you are on your own with God! And you must be true to yourself and your skill set. But I have observed that tenacious visionary leaders, who have clear apostolic and/or prophetic gifts, tend to communicate the vision most clearly and have the passion and tenacity to implement changes earlier than leaders of a more pastoral disposition.

That was certainly our experience at Abundant Life. Paul Scanlon led our small senior leadership team through the reinvention like the sharp end of an arrow. His apostolic wisdom, prophetic vision, personal tenacity and masterful communication skills paved the way. This inspired people like me, with more of a pastoral and teaching gift, to play my part by teaching and nurturing the congregation through the changes. It became a wonderful team effort like all successful church transitions, but without a doubt it was speeded up by Paul's particular gift and personality.

If that makes you wish for a "Paul" to spearhead your own "crossing over," stop it! In our context it worked because God was at the centre of it, but a ministry like his may kill the church in your context. God knows what he is doing and he has put you there to navigate your building process with the other wonderful co-labourers around you. So celebrate your team, don't envy anyone else's and proceed at the speed appropriate for a successful transition in your context.

So, having communicated the vision and then started to make changes, what next?

3. Use the power of a good report

Once you begin to cast the new vision and make some changes, reports will start circulating in the church, team or group you are transitioning. Some will be positive and others negative. Left unattended, the latter will prevail and overwhelm the former. Your third step in the church-building cycle is, therefore, to stop this happening by proactively taking hold of the good reports and putting them to work for you. A good report will always overwhelm a bad report if you use it properly.

This is where creative communication comes into its own. The tools at our disposal today are phenomenal and should be maximised. By all means use the printed page to publish a good report about changes going on in the church community, but in addition use digital media, web-based social media and contemporary audio-visual media.

For example, if having cast your vision you have then made fundamental changes to your youth programme that is generating a range of mixed reports across the church, take some video footage of the event to show to the main church. Include stories of changed lives and interviews with young people raving on about how awesome the new programme is, how easy it is to bring their friends to now and how accessible it has made God seem to them.

Publish a good report. It gets a buzz going, attracts even more volunteers into that area of church life and, most importantly, overwhelms the negative reports that are resisting the change.

I have vivid memories of a few leadership gatherings where this dynamic happened right before my eyes. Not long after we had started our "crossing over" journey as a church there was one such occasion. It was a gathering we had recently invented called "Carry".

This was a new leadership forum for all who were carrying responsibility somewhere in the church. We had taught the church about self-devotion and extended the thought to include the concept that those who carry weight walk differently from those who carry nothing. It became such a strong theme among us that we used it to brand all our leadership gatherings for a period – another small but significant change.

At the "Carry" meeting in question, we had dealt with a number of business items of concern to those present and began explaining some new initiatives we were planning for the coming period. I guess it was vision-casting at a particular level, in that we were aiming to get our wider leadership team on board and envisioned for what came next. All good. Then we opened it up for Q&A from the floor.

What came next was very instructive. One longstanding church member made some very negative comments about the way things were going and Pastor Paul's leadership in particular. Before Paul could respond, up jumped someone else from to floor to say just how effective all the changes had been and told a story of their good fruit. Inspired by his courage, up jumped another in support adding more good report to the argument. More followed and before we knew it, the good report in the room had completely overwhelmed the negative one! It was brilliant to watch. It was the body of Christ in action, good cells in the Body overwhelming negative ones for the sake of the health of the body as a whole.

So as you communicate vision and make your first changes, be ready to use the power of a good report. Then build good reporting in as a regular feature of all you do as a church.

4. Model the new culture yourself

Whatever your role in the organisation, if you have the power to communicate vision, make changes and use the power of a good report, a fourth thing must be happening in the 'church-building cycle': you must be changing. The vision-caster must model the new vision.

It should go without saying that leaders must exemplify all they preach and teach. As is attributed to St Francis of Assisi, "Preach the gospel at all times, and if necessary use words." Our actions speak louder than our words, so your actions in response to the vision you are communicating are paramount. Why should others flesh out the vision if you don't?

For example, if like us you establish that devotion is a core value in the new church you are building, the leaders must be the most devoted. They must been seen devoting themselves to being together, be sharing from the fruit of their personal devotion to Christ, and generally modelling for people what it looks like.

If the vision you cast is of a church that is relevant to its community, one where anyone could come in off the street and not feel out of place, then the leaders must model that. They do it through their choice of words when they preach, making their messages understandable rather than using jargon-filled "Christianese." Their dress code is contemporary. They mix with the crowd and communicate an awareness of the issues the ordinary people of the community are facing.

Similarly, if you preach "empowerment," you have to practice it! But experience shows that true delegation and the empowering of others is relatively rare across the church in the world today.

Many churches are stuck simply because their leaders will not empower others.

At Abundant Life we have empowerment as one of our top three core values, so we have had to become adept at blazing a trail – like all good leaders do – then pulling back to allow others to take things on, empowering them. This is so rewarding when it is done well. The person coming through thrives on the new challenge, and the empowering leader gets to steer their progress while having time to explore new things for themselves. It is a win-win situation. Like Timothy, who was told to "set an example for the believers in speech, in life, in love, in faith and in purity" (1 Timothy 4:12), we must be a living example of the vision we cast and the change we seek as church-builders.

5. Call for agreement
Things are moving now. The vision is communicated, changes are being made, a good report is circulating and all the key players in the organisation are modelling it. The next three steps in the church-building cycle are aimed at keeping that momentum going.

At some point in the process people need to be invited to bring to your collective church-building efforts their "spirit of agreement'. Agreement takes many forms but at core level it is an attitude. It is them saying "I agree," but not always in words. The importance of this cannot be underestimated and for that reason I will return to it further on in this book.

I believe every great church is held together by the "spirit of agreement" found in its builders. They hear the vision explained and their hearts all say "Yes – I agree! I want to help build a church like that." They hear about needs in the community they are building in and their heart says, "Yes – I agree! I will do something about resolving that need." They are with you in heart; their "spirit of agreement" is in the mix when they give finance to a project, serve wholeheartedly or simply turn up for church when they have careers, families and busy lives to lead. Your task as the church builder is to invite that "spirit of agreement" to be expressed in all its various forms, to acknowledge that it exists and to thank them for it.

6. Call for involvement

Agreement is one thing; involvement is another. Some who use lavish words of agreement never actually demonstrate it by getting involved in the building process. So the acid test of true agreement is that people get involved in building alongside you.

Again, this needs an invitation. People need to know how to get involved, where the opportunities are and who to talk to about them. A person should never be able to sit in a church and say, "There's nothing for me to do here." Instead, they should sit there week after week feeling increasingly uncomfortable if they are not involved like everyone else seems to be! I am not talking about guilt-projection here but a healthy atmosphere which effectively says, "The norm in this church is that we are all builders, all contributors, all involved in helping make the vision we have agreed on become a reality."

Skilful church-builders create opportunities for people to get involved in the work, not driven by need but by exciting opportunity. If every week there is an appeal for children's workers, people quickly conclude there are problems in that department and they elect to steer clear of it. But if it is communicated as a vibrant aspect of what you are building together, where increasing growth is demanding more workers who will be properly trained and equipped to change young lives for Christ – people will get involved.

For maximum effect, the call to get involved goes out at two levels: the general and the specific. So far I've described the general: we make broad announcements and create connection points for people to explore serving opportunities.

For example, in one season of our development at Abundant Life Church we produced a booklet called the Directory of Ministries. It was designed to help people discover that there were lots of ways to get involved, something for everyone who had a willing heart and a "spirit of agreement" with our vision. It was always out of date the moment it came off the press because things change so fast in a growing church. But even so, it served as a call to the people to get involved.

In addition to these church-wide general calls, it is amazing how many people respond best to a personal invitation to get involved. From time to time in my home church we conduct departmental MOTs – much like the ones carried out on your car every year. We simply take stock of the ministries progress using the acronym MOT, which for us means Ministry, Objectives and Targets.

Very often this process highlights the need to add into a ministry a particular skill-set or strength. So we get busy thinking our way through the church, putting potential names on the table. Inevitably, many of those names are already busy or key players in other departments of church life. Then, others are great people whom we suspect have something to offer which has not yet been expressed.

Once we are clear about it, we approach people individually to ask if they are open to involvement in that particular area of church life. The joy of seeing their face brighten is unsurpassed. They feel valued. They also feel they can engage in a process with you to find their best fit. The result is that they become more fulfilled as an active church-builder, and the church is enriched through their focused involvement. Never hesitate to ask for people's involvement, be it general or specific. Just always be ready to empower, train and resource them once they do so.

7. Celebrate their contribution
Having called for people's agreement and involvement, the biggest

mistake a church-builder can make is to start taking it for granted. That people willingly give their time, skills, money, love and loyalty to building God's house with you is beyond price. It is the ultimate expression of their agreement and commitment to the cause.

Thriving churches have a culture that honours and celebrates their volunteers. Their volunteer teams are characterised by camaraderie, fun and mutual respect. However, experience shows that this does not just happen. The key leaders must build it into the culture of the church.

Bill Hybels' excellent book, *The Volunteer Revolution*,[9] explores this subject with great insight. He makes the observation that, "A great volunteer culture never happens by accident," and explores key lessons that all church builders need to grasp. I would recommend it to you.

It humbles me just how much we get done as a church with our army of volunteers. It would simply be impossible to do it without them. They are indispensable, awesome beyond words. And they need to know that from time to time!

One way we do this at Abundant Life Church is by ensuring our volunteers have food and drink provided when on a long shift. Our VRS – Volunteer Refreshment Station – serves them sandwiches, drinks and snacks appropriate to their role on any given day. It is a simple way of acknowledging their services and saying, "We know you are here and appreciate what you are doing today."

In addition we encourage our team leaders to do little "Thank You" gifts or events for their people from time to time. Then every year we have a Volunteer Party where our church staff serve the volunteers for the evening. It may be serving food and drink, parking their cars, providing security, or a host of other things the volunteers normally do. It simply says, "We celebrate, honour and thank you."

Part of that evening is an honours-style presentation where we give awards – some serious and some silly – to the best volunteer from each area of church life to loud cheers and banter. It's brilliant fun to celebrate building God's house together in an atmosphere of mutual love and honour. The pinnacle of the evening is our Volunteer of the Year Award – usually given to someone that few have heard of or seen, who has been faithfully working away behind the scenes all year. The unsung hero gets celebrated and the spirit of mutual honour is affirmed as part of our church culture.

All this takes hard work, planning and thought. The pastoral team has to keep this ethic alive and to ensure it does not fade. One of our staff pastors has, as part of her wider brief, the role of Volunteer Pastor. That's how committed we are to not just inviting people to agree and involve in our church but to celebrating that involvement.

8. Keep the prize before them

The vision is communicated, changes are being made, a good report is circulating and key personnel are modelling those changes. The leaders call for people's agreement and involvement, and then celebrate the response by honouring their efforts. Now what? Keep the prize before them.

Throughout the process keep the prize, the end game, the ultimate vision before the people. Remind them often that together you are becoming the fleshed-out church of your vision statement. You are not there yet but in a positive process. Take encouragement from the progress made, tell them about the lives that have been changed, celebrate your achievements and keep the vision before them... all of which should sound familiar to you. Yes, you are communicating vision again!

So, a better answer to the question, "What do we do after steps 1 to 7 of the church-building cycle?" is, "We do it all again!" Keeping the prize before them is vision casting, which takes us back to the start of this church-building cycle. And round and round we go until the building is finished.

All the elements of this cycle must be sustained simultaneously to build a great church. It is not a linear exercise; it is a cycle of enduring elements that together combine to give ever-increasing momentum to the building process.

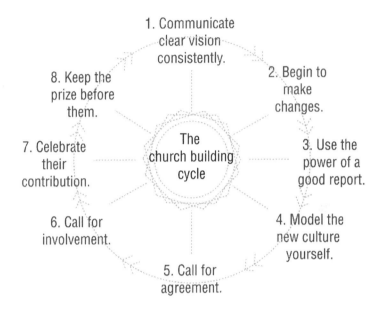

1. Communicate clear vision consistently.

2. Begin to make changes.

3. Use the power of a good report.

4. Model the new culture yourself.

5. Call for agreement.

6. Call for involvement.

7. Celebrate their contribution.

8. Keep the prize before them.

The church building cycle

Wheels within wheels

This cycle of elements is not meant to be an all-inclusive, one-size-fits-all solution. It is simply based on my personal experiences to date, representing vital emphases that need repeated attention as you navigate through the various seasons and stages of building a thriving church. You may well discover that there are other aspects of building the church that are indispensable elements to your process, so just add them in.

All I would ask is that you never forget it is a cycle and not a linear path you travel. In one sense we never stop and move on to the next thing, we just take stock and contemplate how we can do the same things more effectively.

I would like to make one final observation before moving on. So far I have explained the cycle in a church-wide context, but its real power lies in understanding its application in every team within the bigger team that is your congregation. The cycle should be applied to the worship team, the youth department, kids' church and in every community outreach team. It informs our mission to the elderly, the prisons, our staff team, the teams that make Sunday happen and even the executive leadership team and the Board of Trustees.

It functions like wheels within wheels; cycles within the overall church-building cycle we have described. Think for a moment:

• Imagine being in a church where not only the senior team are communicating vision to the church, but all the department leaders are too. Everyone then understands how their seemingly small contribution enriches the whole church you are building.

• Imagine being in a church where positive, progressive change is an ever-present feature of every department, outreach and team. Growth is then attainable, manageable and effective. It is potentially exponential if everyone truly gets it!

• Imagine being in a church where good reports are generated by every single department and team. No divisive, negative or unwholesome reports can survive in an environment like that.

• Imagine being in a church where every person with influence, within every department and team, is modelling the culture and values of the church. People will quickly understand what Christianity is all about and be drawn to living a Christ-centred life in such a saturated culture.

• Imagine being in a team or department where everyone fundamentally agrees and everyone is involved. In that rich atmosphere of mutual respect and serving together, all will feel celebrated and honoured for their contribution, while never actually seeking honour for its own sake.

• Imagine being in a church where every department and team keeps the prize before them, always knowing what it is they are seeking to accomplish for Christ as a team and where that sits within the overall vision of the church they are building.

I want to be in a church like that! And I have committed my life to building one where I live and to helping others build them as I am able in my lifetime. It can be done and, in my opinion, this church-building cycle is at the core of its success once the building has begun.

Chapter 7

The Church God Wants You To Build:
Make It Sticky!

I hope the church you see in your mind's eye and are committed to building is a sticky one. "A what?" I hear you say. Yes, you heard me correctly, "A sticky one."

The concept of what I like to call "sticky church" is something all effective church-builders must understand. The reason is simple: God has always intended his church to be a community that people are attracted to and remain in – that is, they stick. It is a place where people are meant to stay; it has glue! Each living stone is supposed to stick to others; they adhere together in a cohesive unit.

Just think about it, all the biblical pictures of the church we explored in Chapter Two are cohesive, that is, they are images of individuals being held together as a single new entity. The church does not exist because I am a Christian; it exists because that relationship with God places me in a real, living, functioning relationship with you. Only together do we constitute church. As that relationship is worked out we gain cohesion; we look like a building, a family, a flock, a city, a body. And as new believers join our communities, they are supposed to stick and become a functioning part of the identifiable local church we represent.

The early Christians were a sticky bunch. It is impossible to read the first few chapters of Acts and not be struck by the togetherness and cohesion of the new believers. We read statements like:

- All the believers were together and had everything in common (Acts 2:44)
- And the Lord added to their number daily those who were being saved (Acts 2:47)
- They raised their voices together in prayer (Acts 4:24)
- All the believers were one in heart and mind (Acts 4:32)
- All the believers used to meet together in Solomon's Colonnade (Acts 5:12)
- More and more men and women believed in the Lord and were added to their number (Acts 5:14)
- The number of disciples in Jerusalem increased rapidly (Acts 6:7)

These and other New Testament passages amply illustrate that the Church is inherently sticky when healthy. It a place where you are meant to stick, adhere, be glued into. It is the stickiness of church life that makes it hard to drift away from; it holds you in.

Developing a sticky church addresses some of the perennial and fundamental concerns of every church-builder:

- How do we attract people to our church?
- How do we ensure they stick with us?
- How do we make certain that the "back door" is no larger than it should be?

All these issues are issues of stickiness. I hope you are beginning to see why this is an important issue to explore if we are to build effectively. We must understand what is it that makes people stick to the church, the dynamics at work and how we can work with those dynamics in the church-building process.

First let me be clear about one thing. When a person becomes a Christian they are joined to Christ. It is him they stick to, and this is rarely a problem because Jesus is wonderful. However, union with Christ is also union with his people. They are not separate choices.

God made it that way. He also designed things in such a way that the gathered church is his shop window to the world. We are the ones charged with attracting others to Jesus; we make him attractive and influence whether people stick to and become a functioning part of his body in the world or not.

That is a massive responsibility and one that we must take seriously. I believe this is the primary reason why we must build our churches to be sticky, that is, in a way that both attracts people to them and makes them communities they will choose to stay a part of.

So the early church were a sticky bunch, they stuck together and God kept sticking new people to them. As a result they functioned with cohesion, power and authority. That is the kind of church we all want to build. Let's now turn our attention to the factors that, when they are working together, will make a church sticky.

Converging dynamics

Why is anyone attracted to your church? Then once they arrive, what keeps them coming back and ultimately staying with you? These are the issues of stickiness.

I want to suggest that there are three dynamics at work as an individual person approaches your church, each of which contributes to whether or not they will stick. The point where these dynamics converge becomes the point at which a person decides to make your church their spiritual home. These dynamics apply whether the person approaching your church is an unbeliever seeking Christ, or a Christian looking for a new spiritual home. We will explore each in turn before drawing our conclusions, so stick with me.

Dynamic 1
People stick because of things WE do:

By "we," I mean you and I, the existing church members. Whether there are 30 or 3,000 of you, the way we already do church together has a major influence on whether the person who comes to our church for the first time will even return again, never mind stick for the longer term. This is therefore a human dynamic; it is all about the things we do, either by design or default, to make our church sticky.

The potential list of features we could mention here is very long, so I will restrict myself to just seven, which I think are worthy of a particular mention, seven things we all deliberately do to make sure our churches are both attractive and inherently sticky:

1. People stick because of our WELCOME:

We make sure our welcome is warm, friendly and most importantly, genuine. We are hospitable and welcoming at every level.

We ensure everyone understands that this is not just the role of the "Welcome Team" or its equivalent, but is everyone's responsibility. Every person the visitors meet should make them feel welcome: the car park attendants, the information point staff and the Kids' Church workers as the visitors nervously drop off their children. The ushers who help them locate a seat are, of course, supposed to be friendly, as is the person serving the coffee and the team who may end up praying for them.

But we work hard to create a church culture where everyone else is welcoming too. The person they end up sitting next to in the service takes an interest in them, the person they stand next to in the queue for coffee chats easily to them and the person they parked next to cheerily shows them the way if they look a little lost. And if we get it right, this atmosphere of warmth and welcome never appears "put on" or over the top. We are all helpful and genuinely pleased to see them.

This has an impact on visitors. They cannot escape the fact that we are just being ourselves, being real. We are not religious or falsely spiritual but just ordinary people like them who are good to be around and who made them feel welcome. They feel accepted for who they are, not judged, analysed or assessed, just welcomed. And that welcome becomes part of the attraction to visit us again. We did that.

2. People stick because of our WORSHIP:

Every church decides on the form of corporate worship they want to characterise their expression of church. It is an ingredient in the mix of church life that significantly influences the way we build our churches and just how sticky any given new person will find it.

Styles and methodologies abound and there are no right and wrong expressions of worship, just the expression we choose to characterise the church we have decided to build. Some of us go for the pipe organ, others the Hammond organ which continues right through the preaching too. Some opt for "front-led" liturgical forms of worship, while others prefer "congregation-led" spontaneity. The Quakers traditionally worship in silence and some Pentecostals swing from the proverbial chandeliers. My home church has a band, much like a contemporary music group, whilst others have classical orchestras and choirs.

Ultimately what makes worship, worship, is the ability of that expression to bring God and people together in a moment of adoration. The music and guidance from a leader, or lack of it, creates an atmosphere in which people can express their gratitude, praise and love for the God who saved them by his amazing grace. A moment is crafted in which people can connect meaningfully with God, get a glimpse of his greatness and see their life in divine perspective once again.

In such moments things happen. People are set free and they get a fresh revelation of who they are in Christ, while their problems shrink to their true size. The God who is for them causes faith to rise in their hearts, which becomes a platform for fresh vision, hope and breakthrough. There is nothing quite like that moment where God and his people connect in a moment of awesome corporate worship.

But before God turns up we have decided on the form of the worship that will envelop the person new to our church. That is quite a responsibility, but it is something we very deliberately do. Once we have decided what that style will be we all then get busy honing it to perfection.

Some of us work hard to ensure that our style of worship is contemporary, not for the sake of being modern or trendy, but because we believe in the power of expressing the timeless truths of our faith in a worship style that will not feel alien to the new person. One of the worship pastors at Abundant Life Church enthusiastically explained to me just how much he loves the fact that the sound of our worship was not a million miles away from contemporary music styles.

People can be listening to their favourite radio station on the way to church, enter our worship service and find themselves surrounded by music of a very similar genre. As a result they feel some sense of identification because the music is of this age rather than a previous one, and that may make it more likely they will return. Of course all that depends on which radio station they were listening to!

We must all recognise the importance of making our main worship event relevant to the people we are trying to reach and build our church with. So we use songs in which the lyrics are clear and understandable. We ensure the music and singing is played and sung as well as we can do it and mix the sound for maximum effect.

For the same reasons we also deliberately discourage expressions of worship that we feel would disconcert our guests or make them feel uncomfortable. So we may, for example, ban flag-waving, blowing of shofars or the rattling of tambourines in the congregation. We each take appropriate control of the worship in our respective settings because it influences whether people will ultimately stick or not. Again, this is something we do.

3. People stick because of our PREACHING:
We work equally hard on our preaching. In fact we work hard to ensure that all who communicate in any given service do it as competently as possible. This extends from the worship leader who interjects a few words between the songs, to the person who reads a scripture, the one who prays over the prayer requests, the person who gives the announcements and the one who takes the offering. But most of all, the preacher must be good. We do all we can to make sure our preaching is clear, understandable and relevant to the issues faced by the people in the congregation – including the visitors. The language used is everyday language and the tone of voice we use is our normal one, rather than a falsely religious one. The illustrations we use relate to the guest in such a way that they conclude we were speaking just to them.

Our aim is to communicate in a way that brings positive change to people's lives, expanding their view of God, themselves and the world around them. We do our best to ensure they leave our service with tools for life in their hands because when they do, they return for more. Good, relevant preaching contributes to our stickiness. We do that.

4. People stick because of our ORDER:

We all realise that coming to a church for the first time can be a scary experience. The crowd may be large, in which case our visitor can feel lost. On the other hand, if the crowd is small, they may feel they stand out like a sore thumb! But whichever the case, we can put them at their ease by ensuring they walk into a place that is well run, organised and has a pervasive sense of order about it.

Good order makes people feel safe and contributes to our stickiness as a church. Clearly-badged workers and staff make communication easier for our guest and shows we have people in key roles to facilitate a smooth-running event. We ensure each element of the service is appropriately explained so there are no shocks to unsettle them. One little thing we do at Abundant Life Church is to flash each speaker's name on the main screen as they get up to speak, however short the input. It just eases the flow of things for the visitor.

When things seem to go wrong, our visitor needs to feel especially secure. For example, a baby cries in the middle of a quiet moment in the worship, someone passes out on a hot day or is suddenly taken ill. The momentary tension is quickly eased by the efficiency of the first-aiders and the calm reaction of the person conducting the service.

As an inner-city church we sometimes have petty criminals in our service who are looking to steal handbags, purses or other things of value. So we have a low-level security presence – just enough to give a signal to guests that we are watching out for them and just enough to dissuade the culprits. It all adds to the sense of safety and allows people to relax and engage with the service content.

On one memorable occasion at Abundant Life Church as Pastor Paul Scanlon was preaching, a man shouted out something to the effect that he thought the preaching was "a load of old rubbish." The room froze and the tension was palpable. In a calm and measured way Paul took control of the situation, spoke to the church briefly about the individual who was known to us and had him ejected. As four of our stewards carried him out the congregation applauded, not because they bore any animosity to the gentleman concerned but because they appreciated the orderly way it had been handled.

People like to know where they stand; that their children will be safe in our care, their cars will still have wheels on after the service and that that things are well managed and appropriately controlled – without it being over the top. As we do our best to keep order, we contribute to the attractiveness of our church and its inherent stickiness.

5. People stick because of our PURPOSE:

What's it all about? Who is it for? What will happen to the money I give? Why do you help people? All questions that people ask as they approach and start to engage with our churches. So we all work hard to have the answers readily available. In fact, we aim to answer the questions before they have even asked them. Above all else, we make certain they connect with our essential purpose as soon as possible.

People love organisations and events that have purpose. Without a purpose there is nothing to identify with or for them to feel any kind of resonance with. We therefore work hard to ensure that our raison d'être – our reason for being – is clearly articulated in every service by all our people in a myriad of small ways. It is not hidden in the sub-text, hard to find or understand. It is in their face, in a nice kind of way!

On the wall of our entrance foyer at Abundant Life Church we have a number of light boxes carrying images and words that communicate our purpose. They include phrases from our vision statement and core values. We think hard about how we promote things on our website or in printed form to ensure the literature we provide has a purposeful core to every piece of text.

It may be an invitation to an event, a Life Group registration leaflet or literature describing various community outreach ministries.

Modern media is a creative gift to us all as churches. I was at a church recently and as part of the service a short video clip was shown of a lady explaining just how caring her small group had been to her through a tough time. In that two-minute story the purpose of the small group was communicated powerfully by well-chosen words, images and music.

Just last Sunday in my home church a short video was shown of a refugee from Eritrea who had been helped by one of our ministry teams. The tag line was "I was a stranger and you welcomed me." It was powerful and communicated very simply that our essential purpose is to help people in the name of Jesus.

The people approaching our churches are looking for a purpose to identify with, so we must continue to do all we can to make certain it is clear. By so doing we make our church stickier than a purposeless one, or one where the purpose is obscure.

6. People stick because of our INCLUSIVENESS:

Feeling empathy and resonance with our church's purpose is good. But then what? It is very frustrating for new people approaching our churches to see all this purposeful activity but to then feel they cannot get involved in it. If they identify with our vision and want to help make it happen, it should be easy for them to do so.

We therefore get busy communicating to people that "you can get involved here." One of the things I love about my home church is that, within appropriate constraints, a person can come one week and be serving the next. We have created a culture where it is strange to merely attend church, rather than for each person to get involved and play a part in building God's house. If they want to get involved and to feel a functioning part of the mission we share, we make it easy for them.

Of course, not everyone who comes is ready to start giving out straight away; some need to recuperate, find their feet or learn new skills. But they can still get involved as a learner. They can come to a Discovery course, Alpha course, Freedom in Christ course, the prayer meeting, a Life Group, Celebrate Recovery, our Strongstart Bible Study or one of the Thrive relationship programmes we run periodically. There is always something to plug into. Involvement is available and easy to access.

This further enhances our stickiness because it gets people into settings where relationships can develop, and ultimately, it is people who hold people in.

7. People stick because of our HELP:

A pastor friend of mine has a colourful banner in his church foyer with the caption "No perfect people here." His church is creatively reaching hurting people with the gospel and seeing lives radically turned around. He acknowledges that most people first come to his church for help, plain and simple. So he has created a culture where however messed up people are, they smile as they come in because they know they are in good company – we are all imperfect here!

This is, of course, true of all churches, it's just that some seem to be perfect at first glance. But if you stick around long enough the cracks will soon appear, because we are all still on a journey towards Christ-likeness – and most of us have quite some way to go. For this reason the new people approaching our churches need to know they can get help to become better people if they stick around with us.

So we all get busy communicating that our churches are truly places that help people. We point them to a God who will help them and place tools in their hands to help them grow as a Christian. In fact everything we do helps people: our preaching, teaching, worship, advice, prayer support, encouragement, gifts of money or skills or shopping...the list is endless.

The specific nature of the help we offer will of course depend on our resources and size. But even where we cannot help a person we should be able to refer them to someone else who can. We must always function within our competencies to remain credible and within the law. But helping people is what we do because helping people is what God does. And the knowledge that help is available if needed will always encourage people to stick around.

Some may seek to abuse our generosity, and every church has its stories of being taken for a ride by those seeking to benefit from our open-heartedness. So we need to wise up and develop sensible strategies to ensure we help those in genuine need and filter out those with wrong motives wherever possible. That is good stewardship. But even if we do get it wrong, God knows and loves the fact that we are expressing his generous heart to people. So I think it is better to be generous and "ripped off," than to have a reputation for withholding unnecessarily.

A delegate attending a conference hosted at our facility once told us that, having arrived in Bradford he had no idea where our campus was. So he called a taxi and asked for the Abundant Life Centre. The taxi driver replied, "Oh, you mean that place on the hill that helps people?" What a great reputation to have in our city; long may it continue!

Churches that help people are sticky. It brings a whole lot of challenges with it, but if people cannot get help, why would they stay anyway?

So there you have it, seven things that you and I do to make our churches attractive and a place to linger and potentially call home. I have tried to stress that these are things we do; they are the product of hard work, human effort, creative thinking, planning and strategising. That's because it seems to me that too many churches ignore these areas or do a very poor job, and then try to justify their shoddy efforts by appealing to the second dynamic at work as people approach our churches – the things God does.

But I cannot over emphasis this point: what we do gives God a platform for what he does. His Spirit pervades our human effort and makes it supernatural. But if we have not worked with him in a divine partnership, all his wonder, power and grace will potentially be dissipated and made unattractive by our shabbiness. The things we do create an environment in which God can do the things only he can do, and together they make our churches incredibly sticky!

So let's explore the second dynamic that is at work as people approach our churches:

Dynamic 2
People stick because of things GOD does:

The truth is that we can do all the above and more, but unless God shows up, we are just a club with members who share a common interest. However, a great church is not just a social experience, it is a spiritual one. Whilst the "glue" that sticks people to the church has a human element, what makes it really special is its spiritual ingredient, the things God does.

God is beyond measure and can do far more than we can ever ask or imagine. So let me suggest just seven of the things he does as people approach our churches which contribute to their stickiness:

1. People stick because God IS HERE:

How do you describe the presence of God? It is beyond words. The fact is that one of the most powerful influences on people to return to our churches is the felt sense that God is here.

God is here because he lives inside every one of us as believers. We are each individually a "temple of the Holy Spirit" (1 Corinthians 6:19) and when we gather we are collectively "living stones being built into a spiritual house" (1 Peter 2:5) in which God dwells by his Holy Spirit.

We affirm this truth when we gather by speaking and acting as if God is present, which draws the guests' attention to his presence among us. Everything about the service points them to a God who is with us, who is here right now and present in his fullness. The songs we sing point people to God, the testimonies we share celebrate God's intervention in our lives, the sermons we speak bring God and people together in the moment we create.

That God does come among us when we gather is altogether an expression of his grace and his desire to live in the midst of his worshipping people. We cannot create God's presence, it just is. And for that we are forever grateful because without it, our churches would rapidly lose their attraction. Our churches are sticky because God is here.

2. People stick because God MAKES THEM FEEL AT HOME:

The church is a family, God's family. It is a place where we are all supposed to feel "at home." The wonder of it is that such a diverse group of people from all walks of life and backgrounds come together and all feel at home together – only God can do that. If we tried to do it purely as a human society, all the interpersonal and sin-poisoned aspects of human relationships would dominate rather than a sense of being at home together. But when God is in the mix, he makes us feel at home where he wants us to be.

Over the years I have had many new people approach me, sometimes after just a single visit to the church, and say something on the lines of, "The moment I came into the building, I felt at home." What was that? I ponder. How can they say they feel at home with us when they don't even know us yet?

The simple answer is that God did it; it is a spiritual dynamic. He adds people to his church by making them feel at home in a way well beyond any welcome we can humanly create. When people begin to feel at home, they stick, and it is God's doing.

3. People stick because God LIFTS THEM:

As people begin to engage with the church we are building together, they begin to feel better. The words we speak lift their expectations and faith. The atmosphere lifts their spirits and the company lifts their relational confidence. They maybe arrived weighed down with anxiety, worry, guilt, fear or confusion, but they leave with their head held high.

Who did that? Was it our well-crafted service alone? No, it was God about whom the psalmist wrote: "You are a shield around me, O Lord; you bestow glory on me and lift up my head" (Psalm 3:3). It is he who meets and ministers to every person in a way that lifts them to the next level when we gather. And when God lifts people, they come back for more.

4. People stick because God SPEAKS TO THEM:
What is more, out of all that is said to the crowd during one of our services, our visitor comes away feeling some of it was "just for them." In time they will use the words, "God spoke to me" and begin to acknowledge that they had a personal encounter with God.

It may be through a line from a worship song, a comment from a friend over coffee after the service, an aspect of the sermon or a seeming throw-away comment by the person announcing the offering – God uses it all to speak to his attentive people in the room. That is a God-thing, an amazing expression of his desire to help us grow and change for the better. People stick in a church where they don't just sense God's presence but he actually speaks to them.

5. People stick because God gives GRACE TO SEE BEYOND THE CRACKS:
No church is perfect, yet people attach themselves with enthusiasm and commitment to it as their new spiritual family. Like all natural families we let one another down, say inappropriate things, hurt and offend one another – just occasionally and not deliberately, but

it happens. So why would they want to stay in a family like that? I believe it is because God gives grace to people to see beyond human failings – beyond the cracks – to the treasure within each of us. As we forgive one another from the heart, work on our attitudes and draw on God's grace, we experience the truth that "love covers over a multitude of sins" (1 Peter 4:8). Not in the sense of inappropriately putting up with blatant sin in the name of Christian love, but as part of a process of growing together towards Christ-likeness.

If we are sinned against and forgiveness is sought, we extend it and thus our love covers that sin and remembers it no more. We love like God loves, because grace sees beyond the cracks in our character and our faltering efforts to be the person we are destined to become in Christ.

Again, only God can do this. Without his grace permeating our church community, it will rapidly degenerate into a human social club and be riddled with interpersonal issues. God's evident grace makes our churches very sticky.

6. People stick because God DRAWS THEM BACK:

God keeps working on people after they have left our church gatherings in a way we never can – however good our follow-up systems are. As they push their trolley down the supermarket aisle they get a glimpse of someone they saw at church, and it all floods back to them – "That was a good experience … maybe I should go back," they find themselves thinking. They lie in bed and suddenly remember how good they felt after they left the service – that feeling of being lifted was wonderful … "Hmmm, maybe I will go again next week," they ponder. The smell of their next coffee gives them a flashback to the coffee they had after church and the fun-filled conversation that accompanied it.

And so it goes on. God has a way of drawing people back to his house that only he can do. Of course, all our hard work contributed to their positive experience. But we simply gave God a gift to work with and our combined efforts are now making it easier for God to draw them back. We simply "lifted up Jesus" in an accessible and understandable way and God is doing what he promised, drawing all people to himself (John 12:32).

7. People stick because God ADDS THEM

The bottom line, the end game of this process, is that God adds people to his church. As we saw in Acts, "the Lord added" new believers to his church (Acts 2:47; 5:14). This was both universal, in that they were added to the one body of Christ in the world, and local, in that they were added to the church in Jerusalem, or Antioch or wherever they lived. It is the same for us today. Each believer needs to have a sense of being added by God not just to the vast spiritual oneness that unites every Christian in the world today, but also to a local expression of that universal church in their local community: the local church.

What makes the church you or I are building "sticky" to a particular individual is sometimes a mystery. But as we choose to do things God's way and faithfully build in accordance with the vision and commission we have received from him, he will presence himself with us and add to us people to help us build. It is a divine partnership: a combination of the things we do and the things God does.

Finally, let's say something about the third dynamic at work as people approach our church. We are doing all we can do to make it attractive and God is doing what only he can do. What then is the person doing?

Dynamic 3
People stick because of things THEY do:

Every person has their own story to tell about what drew them to a particular church and what holds them in there today – what for them constitutes its stickiness. So I can only deal in broad brush-strokes here. But putting it in a few simple steps it usually looks something like this:

1. They come
Something or someone gets them over our threshold for the first time and they have a good experience. That is because we are doing all we can to make it so, and God is working with us.

2. They come again
So, they decide to come again. Maybe they sense the drawing of God; the divine pull to revisit. On the surface it may be because they have a need they hope we can meet, or they are looking for friends, or answers, or whatever. The important thing is that whether they attribute it to God or man, they are making a clear choice to return.

3. They stick around
Gradually they grow in understanding, get their questions answered and begin to feel at home in our environment. Those who arrived weary get refreshed. The lonely find new friends and those beaten up by life find restoration and healing in Christ. They find fresh purpose for their lives, and like it.

4. They are "devoting themselves"
Sometimes quietly and at other times very obviously, they start to put themselves into the life of the church. Their name appears in a serving rota, they sign up for a Life Group and they register for the next discipleship course on offer. You observe that they are engaging with God in the worship with total abandon and when you speak they are attentive and responsive.

Their name appears on a giving envelope and their lifestyle begins to change. They start to play an active part in building the church with you; they bring friends to church with them and become a functioning part of the body. They are "devoting themselves" to God and his people.

5. They have "stuck"!

The glue has got them! They have adhered to the essence of who we are as a church and have chosen to stick themselves to it.

A divine partnership

My purpose throughout this chapter has been to help you understand that the people we seek to help us build our churches – the raw materials of "living stones" – are only going to come if we first understand, and then get fully involved in what is a divine partnership.

I believe that countless millions of people are looking for God in our generation. They want spiritual happiness and are willing to make a strong decision to attach themselves to a spiritual community that is relevant, credible and contemporary. They are out there seeking the good news that we carry. The lost are searching, the blind are desperate to see and the spiritually dead are craving new life. The issue is, how will we respond?

The appropriate response is to build God's house. We build thriving churches; it is God's ordained way and the only way to fully represent him in the world. That building process is a divine partnership, us working together with God to make God attractive, his people the best they can be and his community the one everyone will want to live in. Great churches don't just happen; they are always a partnership between God and his people. And a great church is a sticky church.

It is about churches like this that Isaiah said:

"In the last days the mountain of the Lord's temple will be established as chief among the mountains; it will be raised above the hills, and all nations will stream to it. Many peoples will come and say, "Come, let us go up to the mountain of the Lord, to the house of the God of Jacob. He will teach us his ways, so that we may walk in his paths." (Isaiah 2:2-3)

The world needs a sticky church. So, whatever kind of church you build and wherever you build it, make it a sticky one!

Chapter 8

The Church God Wants You To Build:

Smash Through
The Ceilings

You don't have to be busy building God's house for long before you will hit one of those mysterious things we call a "glass ceiling." You know how it goes: you have a clear vision, a mission strategy, a developing church culture and a suitable structure. Things start to happen and momentum gathers. People get saved, new people come to help you build, ministries become established and progress is easy to see.

Then it stops! Sometimes this is after a period of almost imperceptible decline, and at other times the halt is dramatically sudden. But one day you find yourself thinking, "What's happened? Why have we stalled? Why have we stopped growing?"

It just feels like you have hit an invisible ceiling. Your observation may be about the whole church or just a department or ministry team within it. But the one thing you know for certain is that you keep bouncing off it. I have to admit that I find those seasons some of the most demanding and frustrating to navigate as a church-builder. I find myself analysing what we are doing because it worked satisfactorily up to this point. What's changed?

The frustration I feel drives me to look at other models of church for clues to smash the invisible, but very tangible, ceiling. I read books on church growth, consider attending another conference on the subject, talk to fellow church-builders – if, that is, I can overcome my embarrassment and dare admit that we have stopped growing. Slowly frustration sets in, self-justification takes over and I convince myself that our growth and progress is qualitative rather than quantitative in this season.

Am I deluded or what? Isn't the church supposed to grow and keep on growing? Our mandate is to reach lost souls and there are millions of them out there, so why aren't they filling my church and contributing to the expression of God's house that I am building?

These and other related questions have spawned a plethora of books and conferences, quite a number of which I have read and attended. Some church growth experts have helped me, others didn't. And I am certainly not setting myself up to be another one by writing this book. But I would be ignoring the "elephant in the room" if I did not say something about it, because it is faced by everyone who aspires to build God's house.

Roof or ceiling?

Even though we aspire to build in a way that accommodates steady, consistent growth in both quality and quantity, all churches seem to grow and then plateau for some reason or another. Our hope is that we can kick-start the growth curve again and at the very least move up to a higher plateau before reaching what we may consider to be our optimum size, because there must be one.

Or must there? That's the tantalising thing. Is it actually possible for any local church to just keep growing until everyone in that community is saved and a functioning part of that local church?

I suspect not, and even the most ardent church growth experts would not tend to see that as the end game.

The fact is, every church is different, as we have been exploring in this book. Every church-builder constructs in accordance with their God-given vision and shapes the culture of that church according to their particular convictions. All are biblically-based but have the personal and local colour that flows from their unique journey and setting. As such, they express one wonderful and much-needed aspect of the multi-coloured and multi-faceted church of God in the world today.

We therefore must accept that there will always been a limited demand for every expression of church that is available in any given community. Not everyone will like the church I am building, and some will prefer to help build another expression of God's house, which may be located just down the road from where I am building. And that is fine.

My challenge is not to be competitive about whose "living stones" those people really are, to covet their success or secretly wish for their downfall. Those attitudes would expose someone who is intent on church demolition and not a church-builder at heart.

Nicky Gumbel of Holy Trinity Brompton and author of the Alpha course, recently reminded delegates at the Stronger Conference – our annual conference for church leaders with the theme of "Building Church, Building team" – that the biblical picture of the church being like a body is not just about the local church. This is where we usually apply its truth, using it to encourage everyone to find their place in the local setting.

But Nicky reminded us that we should also remember that, as God's people, we are one single body in the whole world today – the living expression of the universal church in the earth. And each unique, local church is a member of that worldwide body and vital to its overall health.

It is a challenging view but gets to the root of our insecurities and throws us back onto God's amazing grace that he should chose to be represented by any of us at all. As I sat there, a contemporary "new breed" 21st century church-builder, learning from a successful Anglican vicar, it dawned on me afresh: we need each other to get the job done of being this wonderful, amazing, multi-coloured organism we call the church. Some people in my community will prefer the Anglican church to mine – and so be it.

For that reason alone the church I am building will have an optimum size and I must be at peace with it. The issue then becomes, is my church as large as it should be? Are we at our optimum size? If so, it is not a "glass ceiling" I have hit, it is the roof of the building! And maybe sometimes we confuse the two.

I think the difference between the two – the glass ceiling or the roof – is easy to spot. You can see through a glass ceiling and God's Spirit in you urges you to press through it. On the other hand, the roof is solid and cannot be penetrated.

When you are building God's house within, but near the limits of your genuine capacity, it remains fulfilling work. Even if you hit the roof, you remain happy, because the roof is simply a God-ordained boundary within which he has equipped and resourced you to operate. But if you try to go through the roof, you will become all too aware that you are doing it in your own strength. Your commission as a person and as a church community must be worked out within that boundary for its maximum intended effect. And as long as you do so, your fulfilment as a church-builder is assured.

Hitting the roof does not mean stagnation; rather, there is a peace about things and new strategies begin to emerge about how you can extend God's kingdom further with the resources at your disposal. From a strong local church base, nations of the world can be reached and influenced for Christ. Missionaries can be supported, mission teams sent to projects around the world and specialist ministry initiatives financed and championed. Some churches will plant out new groups that are destined to become local churches in their own right. Others will write songs destined to be sung around the world. After all, the power of a worship song is not related to the size of the church that created it.

In addition, people will come and go because of social mobility, the seasons of their spiritual journey, personal preferences about their best fit in a given local church and other individual factors. And it will all be fine because God superintends where his people are best located at any point in time for his greater good, not ours.

When we are true to ourselves and the church God has gifted us to build for him, a certain peace and confidence comes that results in a church's influence being far greater than what its numerical size may indicate. That's because building the church is fundamentally not a numbers game.

I have often pondered how large we would be at ALC if everyone who had ever been a part of the church had remained with us since our earliest beginnings back in 1975. It would certainly be tens of thousands. So I talk to God about why. If they had all stayed, I reason, people would certainly know about us and we would be on the map because of our size. But then I remember, it is not our job to put ourselves on the map by building a megachurch, but to simply serve the master-builder, Jesus Christ, and construct the church he has asked us to build for a purpose best known to him. Our vision came from him, our mission is his, and our cultural values have been shaped by intimacy with Christ and a prayerful process of foundation-laying. Our structures serve that purpose and we gladly accept that the size and influence of this church is ultimately in his hands, not ours. Unless the Lord builds the house, it is all in vain anyway (Psalm 127:1).

One lesser-known but interesting reason we have fewer people with us than if everyone had stayed with us, is related to a specific word God spoke to us around the time of our "Crossing Over." God told us that part of the uniqueness of our church was that we would be foster carers for some of his people and especially other leaders.

That word to us came at a season when a much-loved pastor joined our staff from another denomination in the UK. Within six months he felt God tell him to move on and return to his previous denomination but into a different role and in a far stronger place within himself. At the time we felt a bit confused because we had a strong sense that God was in his coming and integration into our team. But God spoke to us from Philemon about Paul's role in caring for the runaway slave Onesimus for a season, after which he returned to his master with Paul's blessing. Like Paul, we had been part of the process to get this man of God back onto his true course in ministry, and we would be doing it again.

As a result of this insight and other factors, we hold God's people lightly. Our task is to create an environment in which they can learn, grow, be healed, or whatever they need in their season with us, and then go off to fulfil their commission and extend God's kingdom.

Some years ago a small group from Staffordshire travelled to us regularly as they were unable to find a place to thrive where they lived at that time. I remember meeting with them. Their frustration and desire to build a great church in their area was inspiring but thwarted for reasons best known to Jesus. After a few months they disappeared. Recently I met them again and it all came back to me. They are now thriving as part of the leadership of an emerging church in the region and playing their part in building God's house. All we did was foster them for a season.

Until a couple of years ago, folk filling two cars drove for two hours from the north-west coast to Bradford every Sunday. They even became one of our midweek Life Groups for a season; such was the closeness of our relationship. Then, at one of our conferences, the group leader met a great church-planter friend of ours from a neighbouring town, and the fostering came to an end.

Today that group is a new church, planted out by our mutual friend and God's kingdom is extended. Our commission was to do the fostering; his was to do the church-planting. Together we are the body of Christ in action.

As I write this, names and faces are coming to my mind…pastors who lost their way and needed a place to recover but who are now restored to full health and back leading churches….a former pastor who took time out with us to consider his life and ministry, and is now working in politics and shaping policies for the present government. I could go on.

It is one of life's joys that I keep meeting people, once part of ALC, who are now skilfully building God's house in their part of the world. They were with us for a season: for some that was short and for others many years. But people come and people go in God's economy for a higher purpose than being counted on any particular church's membership roll. That is what God's kingdom is all about! God forgive me for ever wanting to keep them all in Bradford – that would have been a major hindrance to the advance of the kingdom and our personal fruitfulness.

I use these examples to help you see that your enduring influence and contribution to the extension of God's wider kingdom is not limited by your numerical size when you are operating within your God-ordained capacity. A thriving church is both growing and healthy. But just what numerical size that equates to at any time in your history, is for you discover.

Ultimately, the myriad factors influencing a church's size are always related to its personnel, local context and available skill sets. Just know that when operating near the roof, it feels good. However, when you know deep in your heart that you have the potential to be bigger, stronger, more effective and bearing greater fruit, that is the frustration of a church-builder hitting a "glass ceiling." He can see through it to a bigger future but needs skill and wisdom to smash through.

The sharp point

My conviction is that every genuine "glass ceiling" of church growth is shattered by a common element: good leadership. I have yet to experience a "glass ceiling" in my own church, or in that of a fellow church-builder that did not have leadership issues in the mix somewhere.

If you want to smash a large pane of modern glass, you do not take a hammer to it; it will bounce off. You take a sharp point to it and it shatters. I believe the sharp point that penetrates and shatters every "glass ceiling" in the development of your church life and its various ministries is good leadership.

Leaders are the sharp point of the arrow, the diamond tip on the drill bit, the people shaped to tap the ceiling and see it shatter when others have been banging it unsuccessfully for however long. Every "glass ceiling" is penetrated by sharp, incisive leadership decisions. However, it takes the right kind of leader.

Leaders are not all the same. They are each uniquely gifted individuals with skills to lead God's people in particular aspects of the church-building process. What's more, their capacities differ. Just as Moses established leaders of 10, 100 and 1000 as an indication of leadership gift and ability, so some "glass ceilings" will need leaders of a particular style and capacity to smash them successfully.

There can be a complex relationship between incisive leadership and the removal of blockages to growth in your church. So let's explore it by considering some common scenarios that I have encountered over the years. From them we can isolate qualities consistently found in leaders who become that sharp point which breaks the invisible ceiling and ensures progress.

The stubborn leader

The church has reached a plateau. An awareness dawns on the congregation that they are slowly growing old together. The behind-the-scenes chatter is increasingly about the need for change, to do something different, to reach some more people. And it inevitably becomes focussed on the senior leader of the church. What started as polite suggestions from his supporters becomes increasingly public displeasure and lobbying from groups within the congregation. Yet for reasons best known to him and his closest allies, the response is a polite refusal to do anything about it.

Why would any leader not want to be the instrument of change to break the "glass ceiling" that is holding everyone down? For a start, he may not even see the problem and think it is all a lot of noise about nothing in particular. Sometimes fear of rocking the boat or even fear of change itself can grip the heart of leaders and blind them to seeing the need for change.

An unwillingness to make changes that disenfranchise, or displease, powerful people in the congregation can be another reason. Influential family groups and individuals are kept happy because he needs their money to keep things operating.

Personal insecurity about promoting others who may become a threat to his position can also be in the mix. But whatever the rationale behind a leader's decision not to implement changes that would smash that "glass ceiling," he has become stubborn. He refuses to move, to change and to lead the charge as he once did. He has become the cork in the bottle of his own church.

It might happen in a department of church life. Youth ministry can stall as older youths move on into adulthood, and fewer arrive at the younger end to replace them. The vibrancy may have been replaced by a certain predictability and staleness. Bored young people soon become restless, so order breaks down as the restless ones mess about and distract the more attentive ones. And both types slowly slip away, some preferring more exciting settings and others because they hate the disruption to what was once a life-giving event.

When the youth ministry is clearly stuck, it needs incisive leadership to revitalise it and take it to the next level. Perhaps parents start to complain as they pick up on the issues, some even offer help, but all are put back in their place with the message that nothing needs to change. Again, whatever the reasons, what everyone eventually sees is a stubborn leader who has himself become one of the reasons for the endurance of the "glass ceiling."

Leaders who will not lead are a major hindrance to the building process in any church or organisation. The sad truth is that unless they change or move, the building process has to all intents and purposes stopped – and the consequences could be terminal.

Every leader successfully engaged in building God's house must be at heart malleable and open to change. They must be aware of the big picture and refuse to get in the way of what God is building. They need to be people of resolve, able to make strong decisions, but without expressing that quality as stubborn resistance in the face of much-needed change.

The ignorant leader

"My people are destroyed from lack of knowledge" was God's assessment of the state of his people in Hosea's day (Hosea 4:6). They simply did not know the right thing to do. And this may be the cause of the invisible barriers restricting our church-building progress. Indeed, many leaders who acknowledge that a "glass ceiling" exists simply lack the knowledge and wisdom to break through it.

It may be that the leader has never encountered a situation like this before. So it is virgin territory and they need to get fresh knowledge for the new situation. This raises the question of "where from?" They typically turn to their peers, spiritual fathers and mentors for advice, which can be a good thing to do.

But the answer may lie outside a leader's established relationship matrix. Just consider, for example, how many leaders found strategies to reach new people through the Alpha course. It takes some courage and open-mindedness to use material developed in another stream of the church, but we may find the knowledge we seek beyond the borders of our denomination or network.

A few years ago I hit a "glass ceiling" in one of my primary responsibilities, as principal of the Abundant Life Leadership Academy. Though developed in a team context, the Academy is my "baby." I founded it, have steered its development and still believe it is one of the best church-based training programmes available on the market today – but then I'm biased! The ceiling was hard to define but I knew it was there and that unless tackled, it would limit our progress and steadily detract from our students' experience. I needed wisdom to develop the course content, its delivery and our structures. So, my course administrator and I went on a mission to learn from other colleges.

We soon realised it was fruitless visiting ones of a similar size and style to ours; we needed to get out of the box and have an open mind. The journey took us into various streams of the church and to institutions far larger than we may ever be, but we found our answers. The results then took two years to implement into our programme but it has been worth it. Momentum returned because as leaders we were willing to learn.

Ignorance is unnecessary when the opportunity to learn is available. So grasp that opportunity if you need it today. It will take effort and discipline to gain the knowledge you need to smash those invisible barriers, but remember God's promise:

"My son … if you call out for insight and cry aloud for understanding, and if you look for it as for silver and search for it as for hidden treasure…Then you will understand what is right and just and fair— every good path. For wisdom will enter your heart, and knowledge will be pleasant to your soul." (Proverbs 2:1-10)

So, wisdom says, "Go get some knowledge to help you," however earnestly you have to search for it. The answer is out there if you will take simple steps of obedience in cooperation with the Holy Spirit, who will always guide you into the truth you seek. Everything does stand or fall on leadership, so leaders must be the most teachable in the church-building team.

Leaders who smash through the "glass ceilings" of the church-building process are not only willing to change, but are also teachable.

The misfit leader

The "glass ceiling" is there and you accept it is your responsibility as a leader to tackle it. No-one could ever call you stubborn or ignorant because you are observably open-hearted and teachable. Indeed, you are searching every avenue available but to no avail. Having done all you know how to do, the barrier remains. Now what?

I would suggest you may simply not be the leader for that job. You are a misfit trying to be a good fit. The truth is, we all have to come to terms with the reality that we cannot do everything. As we explored in Chapter Four, we all have a NICHE, a spiritual SHAPE which is unique to us, and that shape delineates the boundaries of our effectiveness as church-builders and leaders. Sometimes the barrier just needs a different kind of leader to smash through it.

This is why we must build our churches with a strong team-leadership ethic, one in which every individual is understood and valued for the contribution they bring. Then there then is a good chance that the invisible barrier you are trying to penetrate in your area of church life can be solved with the help of someone else on your team.

I have a number of senior church leader friends who, in terms of primary gifting, are evangelists. So their churches *reach* new people with regularity and effectively but tend to develop a "glass ceiling" around *keeping* those people. They realise they need to be more pastoral if they are to nurture them and disciple them to become all they are called to be in Christ.

So they set programmes in place, try to be more caring and teach series on pastoral themes rather than evangelistic ones, all the while hoping people will settle down with the evangelist as their "shepherd." Gradually they get more and more frustrated and the "glass ceiling" never breaks! Why?

These leaders are misfits when cast in the role of pastors. They would be better off sticking to what they are called and gifted to do, and bringing someone else alongside to be the pastoral person on the leadership team. The "glass ceiling" will soon break and the church will grow as complementary ministries build together.

I know this is a fundamental leadership point, but too many miss it. Insecure leaders who will not work as part of a team soon become blinkered to the fact that some things will never change until another leader gets involved.

I spent my formative church-building years in a network of churches that placed a strong emphasis on the complementary gifts mentioned by Paul in Ephesians 4:11 – apostle, prophet, evangelist, pastor and teacher. Because of that I never aspired to be a senior leader in whom everything was vested, which is bound to keep a church restricted in its development. The willingness to affirm complementary giftings is one reason why the church I have helped build for the last fifteen years has achieved all it has.

Paul Scanlon and I are the two senior guys in terms of age and time together on the journey. Paul is a visionary leader with strong apostolic and prophetic gifts. I, on the other hand, am a pastor and teacher. Our combination has been part of the genius at the core of our leadership team over the years as we learned to respect and submit to each other's gifts. Often I have tried to penetrate a barrier that I was ill-equipped to tackle and Paul would step in and, with his gift, smash that "glass ceiling" in a very short time.

I love the way God uses complementary gifts in the church-building process.

Always remember, it is not being a leader in itself that gives you the ability to smash those "glass ceilings," it is understanding the kind of leader you are. In *Courageous Leadership*,[10] one of my favourite books on the subject, Bill Hybels says:

"I am increasingly convinced that highly effective leaders often have impact not only because they are highly gifted but also because their leadership styles mesh perfectly with specific ministry needs... When leaders are optimally positioned so that their leadership strengths mesh perfectly with the specific needs of the church they can have huge impact. Under their leadership the troops can be mobilized, the mission can be achieved, and the kingdom can move forward like never before."

Each new level potentially has a new devil, a barrier to penetrate, a challenge to overcome. Our task is to get the right leader onto the job so that progress is maintained. Don't be a misfit, be a good fit and watch the glass shatter around you!

Leaders who smash through the "glass ceilings" on their church-building journey are not stubborn, ignorant or misfits. Instead, they are willing to change, teachable and functioning where they best fit, three leadership qualities vital to the church-building process. And just how vital they are will become increasingly apparent as we develop this train of thought in the next chapter. So, read on, church-builder!

Chapter 9

The Church God Wants You To Build:

Penetrating Leadership

Each growth spurt in the church-building process gains a certain amount of energy from having successfully penetrated all previous resistance to progress. Just what that resistance may have been is myriad. But I want to explore some of the possibilities further in this chapter, as well as suggest some strategies to penetrate that resistance.

At one level the battle is spiritual. The resistance we feel comes from the kingdom of darkness, which resists the advance of God's kingdom of light as represented in our church-building endeavours.

This aspect is relatively easy to handle. Scripture makes it clear that in our spiritual warfare, the weapons we fight with "have divine power to demolish strongholds" (2 Corinthians 10:4) and that the one who is in us – the Holy Spirit – "is greater than the one who is in the world" (1 John 4:4).

As we stand firm in the full armour of God we can successfully "take [our] stand against the devil's schemes" (Ephesians 6:11).

From this I deduce that a Spirit-filled, God-centred leader will always win that battle.

The tougher challenge, it seems, is often to do with the human elements that conspire to oppose our progress. I accept that human opposition is sometimes the physical manifestation of a spiritual opposition. But in many cases it is not, because all the parties involved are God-loving, committed Christians who are part of the community we are building with.

My point is that good leaders have to penetrate all manner of barriers, both human and spiritual, that may obstruct the building process at each new stage. And I reckon the human ones cause us more grief than the spiritual ones if we do not anticipate them and then deal with them competently.

As I examine my own journey and talk about the nature of these potential barriers to fellow church-builders who have been "the sharp point of the arrow," I have found many common factors. I want us to examine three of these human scenarios before moving on. This will further equip you to successfully build God's house by becoming a leader who can face these challenges head on and penetrate the resistance they pose to your progress.

1. Competing agendas

The more diverse a church becomes in its ministry expression, the more likely it becomes that subtle forms of competition will develop between the ministry teams. Which ministry gets promoted on church news? Which ministry gets the bigger budget? Which ministry has the best literature? Which ministry is the most fruitful? Left unattended, this competition will undermine progress and become a brake on the momentum of the church.

I recall the time when, as a church, we launched our bus ministry. It got lots of airtime in announcements; reports of its success were everywhere. If you weren't involved in the bus ministry you probably weren't even saved ... or so it felt! Eventually it found its place as just one expression of our outreach initiatives and moved from centre stage.

It was replaced by our "Red Light" ministry to prostitutes, which held centre stage for a while, but then that too made way for the emerging prison ministry. The prison ministry was diverse and effective. The human stories of changed lives became a regular feature of our testimony slots for a season and were woven into our messages.

At that time I remember being pulled aside by the bus ministry co-ordinator who asked me if, as a leadership, we had lost faith for that ministry. "What makes you think that?" I enquired. He proceeded to catalogue how many good volunteers he had lost to the Red Light and prison teams, and how as a result he might need to cut his routes down. "I cannot remember the last time we got a mention from the front," he moaned. But his biggest complaint was that he had been knocked back on a purchase request for some resources, which caused him to suspect his ministry had been demoted in the scheme of things.

By the time we had that conversation the seeds of unhealthy competition were well rooted. I discovered that his attempts to keep certain volunteers in his team had actually contributed to their leaving it. Equally, I discovered that the emerging ministries had been quite predatory in recruiting people without reference to existing responsibilities they may have already had in other areas of church life.

It was a recipe for division and disaster and, more importantly, a brake on our momentum if not addressed. So, as good leaders do, we addressed it by speaking to the teams concerned, getting a better balance in the way we promoted ministries, and making sure the whole church knew that every ministry was important and that unhealthy competition was not going to be tolerated.

You will recall that earlier in this book we established that the vision, mission and culture of your church remain essentially unchanged once correctly established. It is the structure that must remain flexible. On reflection, that is what we did in the situation described above.

The vision had not changed, our mission was still intact and the church culture was being expressed. It was the structure that needed adjusting to accommodate the expansion and to better manage the ministry teams. So simple actions like those I have described, plus putting better reporting structures in place and a decision to employ staff in certain roles rather than rely on volunteers alone, all contributed to our pressing through to a new level of effectiveness.

This is just a modern version of what happened in Acts when the rapidly-expanding early church was faced with the competing demands of its ministry success. We read that "In those days when the number of disciples was increasing, the Grecian Jews among them complained against the Hebraic Jews because their widows were being overlooked in the daily distribution of food" (Acts 6:1). It would seem that the apostles were still involved in the management of that process. But growth was making the system ineffective and unhelpful competition was increasing (Acts 6:2). So, they made a structural change. They initiated a process to empower other competent people in the church and said, "We will turn this responsibility over to them and will give our attention to prayer and the ministry of the word" (Acts 6:3-4).

It was a structural change that got the right kind of leaders in their most effective position for the next season. And the result was: "The word of God spread. The number of disciples in Jerusalem increased rapidly, and a large number of priests became obedient to the faith" (Acts 6:7). Any developing "glass ceiling" was shattered.

Leaders must lead through the challenges of competing agendas at each stage of the church-building process. Not to do so will always create a slow-down in building. So why not turn unhealthy competition into the healthy variety? As the church takes ownership of every ministry expression and celebrates every one of them appropriately, what was once unhelpful competition can become camaraderie and mutual provocation to "spur one another on towards love and good deeds" (Hebrews 10:24).

At one of our recent ministry fairs, where each ministry has a stand advertising their work and people can chat about what they do and how they can get involved, it was pandemonium – of the right kind! There was healthy banter between the stands, efforts to outdo one another with the freebies available, and an air of fun and celebration. You could not enter that hall without thinking, "I would love to be on one of these teams" because the sense of unity and mutual respect was palpable. It was healthy competition and a wonderful contrast to the unhealthy kind.

So, be ready to tackle the challenge of competing agendas as you build God's house. Do not let it slow you down. Instead, penetrate that resistance and take your building to a new height.

2. Interpersonal differences

A second human dynamic that will conspire to stop your church-building efforts in its tracks, is interpersonal differences.

I have celebrated the need for diversity in the leadership team of your church, both in personalities and gifts. But the downside of this in human terms is that we will not always get on with each other. Personality clashes and the management of widely divergent worldviews is the consistent challenge of any growing church's leadership team.

The extroverts clash with the introverts. Task-driven leaders, who just want to get on with it, clash with the ones who want everyone on board before embarking on things. The evangelists annoy the pastors, who just wish they would slow down a bit, and the teachers can't do with the biblically unbalanced statements sometimes made by the visionary preachers. And that's just the leaders! Carry it over into the main body of the church and the mixture is potentially toxic when assessed purely in human terms. Left unattended, it is no wonder churches split.

But we are of course a spiritual people, united by Christ and passionate about God's wonderful plan to reconcile people of all kinds to himself as a unified Body. That takes grace to achieve. The grace we have each received from God we must now express towards each other. As God forgave us, we must forgive others. As God no longer counts our sins against us, so we must not hold a person's past or present failings against them.

Love, grace and forgiveness are the antidotes to the latent toxins of human interpersonal differences. Sometimes we need "tough love" and have to set boundaries within which certain relationships are conducted. And we must always work to resolve differences in accordance with the clear guidelines Jesus gave, which should result in both parties seeking reconciliation (Matthew 5:23-24; 18:15-17).

Where, then, does this leave the church-builder beset with slow progress because of interpersonal relationship clashes? Or more particularly, how can all church-builders build in such as way as to minimise the chances of it ever becoming an issue? Here are a few suggestions.

Create a culture that celebrates differences

Do not be a bland, monochrome church but celebrate the diversity of humankind at all and every level. Have an ethos where it is OK for people to be themselves, soar with their strengths and not be labelled by their weaknesses.

By so doing, you remove the tendency in people to want to be like other people they admire. Instead of them inwardly thinking,

"I wish I was like brother so-and-so," they will start to think "Thank you God for making me, me!"

Teach relational dynamics

Alongside the celebration of our individuality and differences there must be consistent teaching about how to handle relationship dynamics. If we do not teach people to respect, prefer and honour one another, individuals will damage each other and justify it by saying, "I was just being my God-created self as the preacher told me to be."

So into the various forums you have as a church, be sure to drip-feed the biblical principles of love, grace, forgiveness and mutuality. We all need each other. Teach your people how to restore ruined relationships, to build great marriages, mend their rifts and live in harmony with one another.

Part as friends

Some relationship differences will lead to separation. "Such is life," we may say. But some churches have created a culture where to leave any relationship is viewed as a vote against those left behind, especially if you leave the church altogether. But it need not be like that.

Over the years I have talked to many people wrestling with whether or not to move on from one church to another, one ministry team to another, one friendship group to another. Even from one boyfriend to another! Every situation has its own circumstances to take into account, so we must not over-generalise. But we can seek always to part in a friendly and respectful way.

I once made a list of all the reasons people had given me for deciding to leave our church to attend another. There were eleven of them. My question was, "Are they valid? Is it biblically appropriate to move churches for these reasons?"

What they were is irrelevant to my purpose here, but many of them were gleaned from my early days in ministry when we conducted "exit interviews" in an effort to learn from the issues a person was leaving over. With hindsight, it was not a good thing to do. If you invite them to criticise you on departure, they will. And they won't come back even if you subsequently change things to suit them.

The big lesson I learned is that the vast majority of people do not actually leave over an "issue" unless we force them to have one. For most, it is just time for them to move on as part of their spiritual journey. So, if we can release them with grace and dignity, blessing them as they go, they can always return and many do. People will come and go; it's the way life is. Just determine to always part as friends.

But what if there is an interpersonal dispute at the heart of the separation? In those circumstances all you can appeal for is mutual respect and for the parties to seek resolution. And that may end up being an agreement to disagree.

Remember the dispute between Paul and Barnabas? It centred on whether or not John Mark should accompany them on their next mission trip. Paul said "No" because he was unhappy about John Mark's behaviour on a previous mission trip. Barnabas – John Mark's uncle – said "Yes," he was the best person to take with them. They were at an impasse with interpersonal implications.
Subsequently we read that "They had such a sharp disagreement that they parted company" (Acts 15:39). Paul went on his way and took Silas. Barnabas went on his way to Cyprus and took John Mark. They agreed to disagree and parted company.

I like to think they parted as friends. We certainly know that in later years John Mark played a role in Paul's ministry, so if they did fall out the rift was repaired. I also like to think – contrary to some commentators – that both were blessed in their missionary endeavours.

God blesses people, not places, and as each of these men of God had the courage of their convictions to separate as friends, they were blessed. Acts records the blessing Paul experienced. We have to turn to church history to follow Barnabas's journey, but suffice to say, to this day he is the patron saint of Cyprus because he was the one who took the gospel there.

Separation does not have to be negative or counter-productive. Sometimes it is the best thing to happen and God uses it to extend his kingdom as we each walk in obedience to him. So, build in a way that ensures you deal effectively with any potential "glass ceilings" or other barriers to your progress caused by interpersonal differences.

3. Deliberate Opposition

The third and final human dynamic that may rise up to resist your church-building progress arises from those who, for reasons of their own, deliberately set out to oppose your intentions.

Opposition from within

You would ordinarily expect this to come from outside the church but, every so often, you will encounter a person so intransigent that they insist on staying as part of the church whilst resisting all you do. They become a piece of grit in the smooth machinery of your church, clogging processes, resisting change, emitting negativity and generally slowing your progress.

Incisive leadership deals with that kind of person with "tough love," marginalising their influence and if necessary identifying them as a trouble-causers (see 1 Thessalonians 3:14-15). In extreme cases it is appropriate to excommunicate them after an appropriate process, in line with biblical teaching on how to handle a divisive and persistently unrepentant person (see Matthew 18:15-17; Romans 16:17; Titus 3:10).

I hope you never have to work such a process. I have only had to do it a few times in my 30 years of ministry. But if it comes your way, deal with it quickly. Not to do so is inviting trouble to remain in your world and accommodating a factor that will slow you down. That will violate your church-building aspirations and mandate from heaven. So bite the bullet and lovingly, but firmly, deal with the problem and get on with the building.

Opposition from outside

External opposition to your church-building aspirations is what you are more likely to expect. We are all aware that not everyone rejoices when the people of God thrive. Our light exposes their darkness and in response they may conspire to oppose our desire to build God's house.

Many years ago the local Pagan Society picketed our church in Bradford. We were engaging in a series of outdoor projects that included music, speaking, activities for children and so on. They positioned themselves with placards right in our face and sought to stare us out. It was freaky!

We have had incognito newspaper reporters in our services asking awkward question of people to try and get an angle on us. We have been systematically trashed by one tabloid newspaper and had a range of disgruntled citizens complain to the authorities about us. Every single accusation and consequent investigation came to nothing, because there was nothing to find. But things like that do become massive distractions from the church-building process if you allow them to be.

However, we must not build with a disproportionate expectation that we will be opposed. After all, Scripture teaches that "when the righteous prosper, the city rejoices" (Proverbs 11:10). I prefer to live with that expectation!

Whenever faced with external opposition I always refer to my friend Nehemiah. His story has so much to teach us about how to build the community where God dwells. You will recall that he was given leave to rebuild the walls of Jerusalem by his master, the King of Persia. Persia also controlled the surrounding territories, the local rulers of which had a vested interest in what happened in the region around Jerusalem.

Sanballat governed Samaria to the north, Tobiah governed the areas of Ammon and Trans-Jordan to the east, and Geshem led a coalition of Arab tribes to the south. All three were therefore politically opposed to the emergence of a revived kingdom of Israel because its success would potentially threaten their power base. Geshem also controlled the lucrative eastern spice routes that passed through Israel to the sea. So Israel's emergence was also a potential threat to his trading activities.

It is not surprising, therefore, that these unspiritual men sought to oppose Nehemiah's work of rebuilding Jerusalem. From their attempts we learn two important things: the ways in which external opposition may come to thwart our church-building efforts, and the best ways to counter it.

Each of their five attempts to oppose the building process increased in severity and complexity, but you know the end of the story – the walls were built in record time (Nehemiah 6:15-16). So take heart, no external threat need thwart or even slow down your church-building efforts. Just learn from Nehemiah and watch out for:

a) Insults
The moment the building started the opposition began. It came in the form of low-key abuse and insults, just enough to register displeasure (Nehemiah 2:18-19). They poked fun at God's people, implying they were breaking the law in what they were doing, a groundless accusation.

Nehemiah's response was swift and concise: "The God of heaven will give us success. We his servants will start rebuilding, but as for you, you have no share in Jerusalem or any claim or historic right to it" (Nehemiah 2:20). He basically told them to keep their nose out – it was nothing to do with them. He also affirmed that it was God they were serving.

Never forget that unspiritual people have no place in shaping, commenting on or making decisions about the spiritual project you are involved with. It is God's house you are building and you only take notice of what he says. So, do not let any insults slow you down.

b) Incitement

Next, the opposition went up a gear. Insult and mockery turned to anger. "When Sanballat heard that we were rebuilding the wall, he became angry and was greatly incensed" (Nehemiah 4:1). Further insults followed in an attempt to incite Nehemiah to do or say something he would regret. That anger then turned into a deliberate plot to incite trouble: "They all plotted together to come and fight against Jerusalem and stir up trouble against it" (Nehemiah 4:8).

Nehemiah responded superbly. He prayed and did not even engage the enemy in conversation. As the threat increased they "prayed to God and posted a guard day and night to meet this threat" (4:9). So, sensible precautions were taken after which we read: "I stood up and said... 'Don't be afraid of them. Remember the Lord, who is great and awesome, and fight for your brothers, your sons and your daughters, your wives and your homes'" (Nehemiah 4:14). He reminded everyone of the big picture, the context they were building in.

There is great wisdom here and I would suggest you read the whole of chapter 4 if you ever find yourself in this kind of situation. The overriding lesson is that Nehemiah just did not get into it with the enemy. He simply prayed, took sensible precautions and reminded everyone why they were building. As a result the building work did not stop or even slow down because the enemy's divisive tactics had no ground in which to take root.

Having failed to stop the building through their general broadsides of insults and incitement, their tactics changed. They turned on Nehemiah in particular, no doubt reasoning that if they could take the leader out, everyone else would stop what they were doing. Leaders, note this well, because what follows could come your way. It can be very subtle in its approach but do serious damage to your church-building progress.

c) Isolation

They first hatch a plan to isolate Nehemiah from the building work (6:1-10) sending a letter inviting him to a meeting well away from Jerusalem. He realised that they were scheming to harm him. So he sent this reply: "I am carrying on a great project and cannot go down. Why should the work stop while I leave it and go down to you?" (Nehemiah 6:4). He resolutely refused to be drawn away from his fellow builders, even when the enemy persisted. Four times they sent the same message and four times Nehemiah replied with the same response. Then it arrived for a fifth time with a top-level emissary and a letter explaining there was a rumour Nehemiah was setting himself up as King of Judah, so they needed him to come and explain his intentions.

It was all an attempt to isolate the leader from his people. Nehemiah's reply is simple and robust: "Nothing like what you are saying is happening; you are just making it up out of your head" (Nehemiah 6:8). And he got on with the building.

The lesson for leaders here is: do not let anyone isolate you from your building environment. Invitations will come, I can promise it. "Come to a meeting," "Please come and explain yourself," or similar requests will come from people who are fundamentally opposed to what you are building. They should be carefully weighed and most probably ignored. Do not leave what God has called you to build.

A lesson from church history springs to mind. During the years after the Reformation, Martin Luther was repeatedly summoned to Rome by the Pope to explain his reasons for rejecting Catholic doctrine and leaving the Roman Catholic Church. He refused to go, realising he would probably never get home alive. He remained in Germany, where he was building.

But an earlier pioneer of the day, who greatly influenced Luther, did take up such an offer. John Hus, from Prague, was promised safe conduct if he would come and explain himself to the papal authorities. He went but never returned home.

If you are building a family, you need to be there. If you are building a business, you need to be there. If you are building a ministry, you need to be there. And especially if you are building the most important building in the world – God's house – you need to be there. So do not let an enemy isolate you, however plausible their reasoning may seem to be.

d) Insulation

Having failed to isolate Nehemiah they next tried to insulate him. They couldn't extract him from the project, so maybe they could trap him within it (Nehemiah 6:10-14). The sneaky part of this ploy was that it came in very spiritual-sounding terms.

Nehemiah was invited to meet with a false prophet – who delivered a message that he should lock himself in the temple because men were coming to kill him. Again, Nehemiah realised what was going on and replied, "Should a man like me run away? Or should one like me go into the temple to save his life? I will not go!" (Nehemiah 6:11).

He then explained, "I realised that God had not sent him, but that he had prophesied against me because Tobiah and Sanballat had hired him. He had been hired to intimidate me so that I would commit a sin by doing this, and then they would give me a bad name to discredit me" (Nehemiah 6:12-13).

This sounded really spiritual: "Let's hide away with God." But it was actually contrary to God's word because only priests were allowed inside the area he was suggesting. There was an altar of asylum situated in the public area of the temple courts (Exodus 23), but this inner area was forbidden to Nehemiah, and to go there would have ruined his reputation.

The key here is, never lock yourself away with anyone who is not building with you. Stay on the wall! Too many of God's people get caught by this one: they lock themselves away for so-called spiritual reasons and stop actively building God's house, not realising it is an enemy tactic to insulate them in a spiritual cocoon well away from effective building.

Think carefully before getting over-absorbed in doing the Christian conference circuit, taking time out for inappropriately long periods of seeking God, or being drawn into symposiums and debates on theologically deep but practically worthless topics. Only leave the building to gather what you need to help you continue building.

Never be isolated away from the task and never insulate yourself in spiritual cotton wool from the task. Be like Nehemiah, pray as you build, read as you build, study as you build and get counsel as you build. That's what penetrating leaders do.

e) Intimidation

No doubt exasperated by their failure to stop the building work through their insults and incitement of the people, and then their attempts to isolate and insulate the leader himself, Tobiah made one last attempt to influence Nehemiah. He used intimidation – but in a very interesting way.

The wall-building had just been completed (Nehemiah 6:15) and Jerusalem was now secure. Nehemiah was about to turn his attention to repopulating the city and other matters, further strengthening the economy and influence of Israel. Because Nehemiah had successfully completed his primary task, Tobiah, his enemy, now decided that the best way to influence Nehemiah was to become his friend. He did this by targeting people with divided loyalties and asking them to speak well of him to Nehemiah. Those same people spoke to Tobiah about Nehemiah, becoming a conduit for manipulation and deceit. But again, he saw through it all. He saw the private agendas that were creatively camouflaged by the litany of letters and reports that were circulating. His conclusion was that Tobiah was trying to intimidate him into being his friend (Nehemiah 6:16-19).

This teaches us that we must be careful who we listen to and who we talk to. If enough people who seem to be "for you" speak highly of your enemy, you may start to believe them and end up in an inappropriate liaison with him. I don't want to make you cynical or less trusting of people. But I do believe the enemy is subtle and if he can use people close to you with divided loyalties to get to you, he will.

Nehemiah realised there was one simple way to avoid all this. He put people he knew he could trust in positions of power and responsibility on his building team. Not just people he liked but people he knew were godly and of good character.

The very next verses tell us about the man he put in charge of the citadel and the man he put in charge of the wider city. His reason was clear: "...because he was a man of integrity and feared God more than most men do" (Nehemiah 7:2). Surround yourself with people like this and you will never be tempted to give in to the subtle pressure to be friends with people who, you suspect, are really your enemies – wolves in sheep's clothing.

In the last two chapters we have considered a range of factors that conspire to slow down or halt the church-building process you are engaged in. Whether it is dealing with "glass ceilings," or confronting the challenges of building with "living stone"' and the human dynamics that brings to the process, I pray you will have the resolve to stay on the wall and build until the work is complete.

Chapter 10

The Church God Wants You To Build:

Holding It All Together

My mobile phone rang. The display showed the caller was a long-standing pastor friend, so cheerily I answered. But his greeting was audibly tense.

"What's going on mate?" I enquired.

"It's all falling apart!"

"What is?" I asked.

"The church," he said. "I just can't believe it. After all we've been through and built together, it just seems like it's all unravelling around me and I don't know what to do."

My heart sank for a moment as I empathised with his anguish, and then quickly revived as we switched into problem-solving mode. The discussions, meetings and strong decisions that followed that first cry for help saved his church from major fragmentation. But that is not always the case.

Why is it that having set out to do all the positive things we have explored in this book so far, a church can suddenly unravel? Sometimes a minority with a loud voice end up leaving before peace returns. More serious cases may result in a church split. And in the worst cases the church completely disintegrates, scattering its "living stones" in every direction.

Some of these will, no doubt, be used in other church-building projects. But many, sadly, remain disconnected and damaged by the process, never again to play a significant part in building God's house. My heart aches for those people.

I believe that, as church-builders, we should do all in our power to avoid causing such damage. Also, wherever possible we should be open to being used by God to re-gather such scattered "stones," so they can be repaired and restored to significance in a glorious expression of God's house.

The key to avoiding these terrible scenarios – or at least to spotting them approaching, thus allowing time to take preventative measures – is to understand the dynamics that hold a church together. I am suggesting two main principles, or dynamics, that all church-builders need to be aware of. Together they constitute the glue, or bonding agent, that keeps a church cohesive. Both have already had a brief mention in this book but deserve a fuller exploration.

Building agreement

I have project-managed a number of church construction projects over the years, the most recent being a significant extension to our main building called the Champions Centre. One day, back in 2007, I received a call from my assistant to say the quantity surveyor had arrived with the contract for the work, which was ready for me to sign.

Into my office he walked but was empty-handed. At the very least I had expected him to be carrying a briefcase or large envelope for me. So I said, "I thought you had the contract with you?" "I do," he replied. "Here it is." And following behind him staggered one of his assistants with two obviously heavy boxes – the kind you bulk-buy photocopier paper in. Thud! They landed on my desk. "There you go," he continued, "There's one for you, one for the contractor, and one for me."

That contract was our building agreement. It was hundreds of pages long and contained every drawing to be used in the construction. It listed every nut, bolt, screw and fixing to be used in the build and, most importantly, it described the contractual responsibilities of all the parties to the contract.

It was a monster! But that contract saved our building project from grinding to an untimely halt when the builder later got into difficulties and eventually ceased to trade. It saved us both money and time, because it contained an agreed basis for what would happen in such circumstances. From that I learned an important lesson: every successful building project needs a building agreement.

What is true of a natural building is also true of the spiritual one. To effectively build God's house, there needs to be a building agreement between the parties. Of course, no-one is ever going to sign their life away on a document equivalent to the one used to illustrate my point above. And neither should they. The agreement to build God's house is a far less concrete thing in written terms, but just as substantial in spiritual terms when understood and entered into with faith. In that we are building a spiritual building, the agreement we need is a spiritual one, not a physical one.

To the terms of that church-building agreement – which we will explore below – we each bring our personal "spirit of agreement." And I believe that this is the single most important thing each fellow-builder brings to the church-building process.

It was a "spirit of agreement" that unified the builders of the Tower of Babel, and it made them unstoppable in human terms (see Genesis 11:1-9). People "walk together'" – or in our context, "build together" – because they have agreed to do so (Amos 3:3). Jesus said that "If two of you on earth agree about anything you ask for, it will be done for you by my Father in heaven" (Matthew 18:19).

There is great power in agreement, especially when it is an expression of God's will. No wonder, then, that Paul's appeal to the fragmenting church at Corinth was: "That all of you agree with one another so that there may be no divisions among you and that you may be perfectly united in mind and thought" (1 Corinthians 1:10).

The terms

To understand what the likely terms of such a church-building agreement might be, we need to return to my church-building hero, Nehemiah.

Nehemiah and his fellow-builders model what can be achieved when there is a building agreement in place. Remember, they were building the walls of Jerusalem, the city where God lived, just as we are building the church, which is where God lives by his Holy Spirit today. So their experience has much to teach us as modern church-builders.

I have observed that there are at least four key terms in the notional building agreement between Nehemiah and his fellow-builders, each of which has its modern equivalent for us today.

Term 1 – We all feel what God feels

Jerusalem was in a mess, devastated by the Babylonians. And even though God's people had been allowed to return and rebuild the temple, it was still a shambles in terms of being a cohesive community that truly reflected the glorious God of Israel.

Based on the reports that first reached him, Nehemiah described Jerusalem as being "in trouble and disgrace" (Nehemiah 1:3). And when he eventually arrived to survey the city for himself he exclaimed, "See the trouble we are in: Jerusalem lies in ruins, and its gates have been burned with fire. Come, let us rebuild the wall of Jerusalem, and we will no longer be in disgrace" (Nehemiah 2:17).

Note that he uses the words "trouble" and "disgrace" again. He realised that a city without walls lets things in that should be kept out. There was no distinction between its inhabitants and outsiders, no protection from enemies, no boundaries to define appropriate limits for people – which all results in a community in trouble and disgrace.

It is reminiscent of the proverb that says: 'Like a city whose walls are broken down is a man who lacks self-control' (Proverbs 25:28). Without the walls of self-control in place, a person ends up in trouble and disgrace. And Jerusalem had become a practical illustration of that enduring principle.

This situation grieved Nehemiah. That the dwelling place of the one true God of Israel was in trouble and disgrace moved him deeply. I believe that what he felt was what God felt. And it was those deep feelings that moved him to act on God's behalf.

Recalling his response to the initial reports of the mess Jerusalem was in, he writes, "When I heard these things, I sat down and wept. For some days I mourned and fasted and prayed before the God of heaven" (Nehemiah 1:4). The following verses are his impassioned appeal to God to help him be part of the answer. He felt something and he felt it deeply.

The next day he went to work in the palace and was visibly gloomy. So much so that the king asked him, "Why does your face look so sad when you are not ill? This can be nothing but sadness of heart" (Nehemiah 2:2). He explained the problem and, as a result, he was dispatched with the king's support for the rebuilding work.

Nehemiah built for one simple reason: he felt what God felt. He cried the tears God was shedding about the state of his community. It moved him to action, to find others of like mind and to initiate the adventure of rebuilding.

Feeling what God feels is the first stimulus that must galvanise us as we set out to build God's house together. We must find an agreement that together we feel what God feels about our community — its people, its problems, its politicians, its local complexities, and especially the state of the church we are building.

In the early days of our proactive outreach into the more deprived areas of Bradford's inner city, our feelings as a church were tested. Did we really feel what God felt for the poor and disenfranchised we found there? Or would our socially conditioned middle-class prejudices get in the way? Thankfully, God's heart prevailed — but not for everyone. Some did not feel what God felt and so chose to part company with us rather than risk their children sitting next to a drug addict or prostitute in one of our meetings.

I also recall when our church first started to broadcast its services on Christian TV. It was a high-profile venture involving significant set-up costs and the church rallied around it — for the most part. The need to produce an initial run of programmes for the broadcaster resulted in our holding back-to-back services just to get ahead of the game. It was one of those all-hands-on-deck situations and we had a lot of fun with it.

But there were a few notable absentees, leaders of some influence in the church. Eventually they surfaced to make it clear they felt the whole TV venture was misguided. Matters were further inflamed when they discovered that the new auditorium we were in the process of building was to have very little natural light. This was to allow for creative lighting in the stage area but they saw it solely as us building a TV studio.

Feelings ran high and, however much we talked, they never came to peace. We felt God was opening the way for us to use TV to communicate our message with an audience we could never reach in a lifetime of travelling and conference speaking. Failing to feel what we believed God felt about the project, they left.

Everyone on your church-building team should feel what God feels about the kind of church you are building together. When they hear the vision explained, their hearts all say, "Yes – I agree! I want to help build a church like that." And it extends to every aspect and expression of the church we are building together. When we do, our bond is strong.

Ultimately, what you feel in your spirit will determine what you will do and when you will do it. So ask God to give you his eyes and his heart for the community you are building in.

Term 2 – We will all get involved in the building

It is often noted and quoted by those with an interest in church-building dynamics that there is an 80/20 principle at work in many churches. Eighty percent of the work is done by twenty percent of the people. This has been drawn from business and management circles where it is called the Pareto Principle – named after the Italian who first observed and documented its frequency in life.

This "law of the vital few," as some call it, is certainly present in many churches in the world today but should never be allowed to define them. Indeed, to let it do so violates the very essence of the church. The nature of the church is such that every "living stone" has a part to play, and only as they do so are we at our most fruitful and effective.

People's reasons for treating the church more like a shopping experience – as a consumer – are many. But they are never valid. Only an attitude that says, "I am here to contribute" makes building church the mutually rewarding experience that it should be. That "spirit of agreement" to help make church happen results in everyone getting involved with the church-building process.

This is exactly the kind of agreement we see modelled by Nehemiah and the people of Jerusalem. People from all walks of life came together to ensure the walls were rebuilt. There was no posturing over who got to do the most visible or important sections.

There doesn't even seem to have been a skill-specific allocation of labour. Instead, what we see are people working together, galvanised by their agreement to rebuild the walls, and just doing what needed to be done.

Chapter Three of Nehemiah is the account of who built where on the wall. For that reason it can appear tedious at first glance – just a list of names and where they built. But a slower read reveals some interesting factors that need to inform our modern church-building endeavours. For example:

Building is all-inclusive
The list of people working on the walls included willing men and women from all walks of life. We read of priests, rulers, merchants and temple servants all working together. Even goldsmiths and perfume-makers were involved – not the most obvious trades to have on a building site. But that's the point. It wasn't about withdrawing from the process until a perfume-maker was needed. The perfumier just had a desire to help build and got stuck in doing what was needed.

I love that kind of selfless commitment to building God's house. It reminds me of a senior cardiac surgeon who used to wash up in our café area after each service. And a friend of mine who manages a team of over a thousand lawyers in his day job, but gives the church a day a week to support people pastorally in the community. Their heart is simply to serve the vision we share. It flows from an agreement to get involved with the work – whatever it happens to be this week – and characterises all thriving churches.

Building starts where you live
Just why a particular person rebuilt the section of wall they did is not explained, except in a few cases. I like to think those cases are typical of the rest. We read: "Jedaiah ... made repairs opposite his house" (3:10) and "the priests made repairs, each in front of

his own house" (Nehemiah 3:28). Also that "Zadok...made repairs opposite his house" (Nehemiah 3:29).

So, we have people building where they lived. That is exactly where building God's house starts today, in the community where you live – your street, office, classroom, local gym or factory. It is there that we work to gather the "living stones" and craft them into the community of God's people we call the church.

As a pastor I get asked to do a lot of character references for people in our congregation. They typically include job applications, training courses and missions trips. I am always honest, which sometimes gets me in trouble!

On one occasion a reference request arrived for a young man who had applied to go on an urban mission trip to the USA. I was perplexed and a little dubious about his motives because, here in Bradford, he was not helping or reaching anyone as far as I could see. He was denied a place by the charity concerned and he blamed me! So we had to have a pastoral chat about the fact that you don't have to go on a mission trip to reach people; you just have to step outside your front door.

There were no gaps in the building
As this random group of individuals each outworked their agreement to play their part in the building process – getting involved right where they lived – the walls were eventually rebuilt. And there were no gaps. The list of workmen starts with those rebuilding the Sheep Gate and ends at the same place (Nehemiah 3:1, 32). So it went full circle.

This is a wonderful picture of how we should build the church today: everyone playing their part so that there are no gaps for people to fall through or enemies to enter by. This only happens when everyone agrees to get involved in the building and takes their church-building contribution seriously.

When they don't, their absence creates a gap and potential vulnerability. That's why everyone needs to be in this building agreement!

There were no isolated builders
The most repeated phrase in this chapter is "next to." Everyone built next to someone else. There was someone on their left and someone else on their right. Everyone was connected. There were no isolated builders, working on a part of the wall away from everyone else. And that is how it should be as we build the church today.

Our connectedness is crucial to our success. We need each other's friendship, encouragement and support to accomplish the task. Indeed, experience teaches us that isolated builders are a danger to both themselves and the interests of God's kingdom. They are easily deceived, attacked or rendered ineffective. Our power is in our agreement to build together, which means actually being together. Only then do we experience the many benefits of mutual support, accountability and shared success in our church-building work.

Agreement means nothing until we get our hands dirty! So we must develop church cultures where it is unacceptable for twenty percent of the people to be producing eighty percent of the fruit. Church-building is team work in its fullest sense.

Every single person is on the construction team. So, like Baruch, who "zealously repaired" his section of the wall (Nehemiah 3:20), let's enthusiastically play our part. Then, as we periodically reflect on our progress – as Nehemiah did when the walls were half way up – we will also be able to say that this was achieved because "the people worked with all their heart" (Nehemiah 4:6).

Term 3 – We will respond to God's word as one
Things happen quickly when God's obedient people respond in

unity to his word. Nehemiah's story amply illustrates the point. The walls were rebuilt in just 52 days, an amazing achievement to onlookers, who had to agree that "this work had been done with the help of our God" (Nehemiah 6:15-16). Where we all agree to respond to God's word as one, he comes alongside and multiplies our efforts. Therein is the power of agreement with God.

I must, however, draw your attention to an important distinction we need to make in this story. Responding to God's word about a project – like rebuilding the walls – is one thing, but responding to God's call to change the way we do life every day is another. The former is an event, the latter, a life-long process. But each is equally God's word to us.

The contrast between these two types of word from God is well illustrated by Nehemiah's story. God's enduring word to his people Israel was enshrined in the law of Moses, regulating every aspect of their life and conduct as his chosen people. That agreement between God and his people – which was covenantal in nature – also carried with it wonderful promises of blessing for their obedience, as well as curses if they wantonly disobeyed him (see Deuteronomy 28). Indeed, it was disobedience to God's word that had resulted in the overthrow of Jerusalem and exile to Babylon, prior to the events of Nehemiah's day.

Nehemiah and his fellow-restorer, Ezra, realised that this was the big picture within which their respective building projects sat. So, whilst it was wonderful to see God's willing people all pulling together in response to the call to rebuild the city, they knew there was a bigger agreement required if this generation were not to repeat the folly of their forefathers.

I have seen this mirrored in many modern church-building projects because we, too, operate at both these levels today. God may speak to a church about a specific initiative and everyone gets behind it. The enthusiasts spur the initially reluctant into action, and after the event it can truly be said that as a church they had all responded to God's word as one. Meanwhile the big picture for that church remains slow growth or no growth, even decline, because of a widespread failure across its congregation to respond as one to God's wider, more enduring word. For us, that enduring word is the new covenant as enshrined in the pages of the New Testament. In it we find the principles God requires his redeemed people to live by, principles that govern every facet of our lives as his people.

So, a congregation can all agree to rally around a new construction project, the launch of a new ministry or the purchase of a new vehicle – all short-term projects. But at the same time they can be tolerating immorality, failing to deal with divisive gossip, wrongly preferring people or committing a host of other sins. It is such violations of God's wider word that will cripple and slowly kill a church, however much its people pull together around a short-term project.

This awareness should cause us, as church-builders, to teach our people about the need to live in both personal and corporate agreement with God's word. This will mean long-term blessing, health and prosperity for our churches. It is an agreement to keep that word which holds a church together.

Understanding this distinction, Ezra and Nehemiah set about ensuring the people knew exactly what God's whole word was. And the truth slowly dawned on them. As Ezra and his fellow-Levites instructed them in the Law of Moses, they began to respond as one people and united in an agreement not to repeat the sins of their fathers (Nehemiah 8:1-17). The result was, "Their joy was very great."

The more this revelation dawned on them, the more they wanted to affirm their desire to collectively live God's way. So, they repented publicly and, as one people, declared: "In view of all this, we are making a binding agreement, putting it in writing, and our leaders, our Levites and our priests are affixing their seals to it" (Nehemiah 8:38).

The next verses list those who put their seal on the agreement –
and Nehemiah was first, as ever, leading by example. And it closes
by saying: "All these now join their brothers the nobles, and bind
themselves with a curse and an oath to follow the Law of God
given through Moses the servant of God and to obey carefully all
the commands, regulations and decrees of the LORD our Lord"
(Nehemiah 10:29).

In other words, they entered into an agreement to respond to
God's word as one – God's full word as contained in the Law of
Moses, not just a short-term, project-specific word. This was the
basis of their future blessing. All they had to do was live it out
on a daily basis, just as we have to walk in the terms of the new
covenant as God's people today. Ultimately, the joy and blessing
they experienced was not because they rebuilt the walls. It was
because they committed themselves to daily obedience to God.

To effectively build God's house today, we first need each
individual to be walking in daily personal obedience to God's
enduring word. That is the big picture, and the essence of our each
agreeing to respond to God's word as one. Then, from time to time
we need a collective agreement to respond as one to any project-
specific words.

What we must never do is allow those short-term projects and
the momentum they bring, to replace our more fundamental
agreement to live God's way. To do so would be like putting a
sticking plaster over a cancer in the body. And, however many
plasters you conjure up – in the form of creative projects for people
to rally around – without that deeper agreement to all respond to
God's abiding word as one, the church will not hold together.

Term 4 – We will protect our building agreement
In the three terms of agreement above, we have what I would
consider to be the essence of Nehemiah's building agreement with
his people.

Their success was vitally related to their shared ownership of, and agreement to outwork, these dynamics:

- We all feel what God feels
- We will all get involved in the building
- We will respond to God's word as one

I also believe that it takes a similar building agreement to galvanise the diverse people and interest groups that exist in every local church today. This will, no doubt, be expressed in words and ways appropriate to each local context. But its importance lies in being a crucial part of the glue that holds everyone together. Without an agreement you will fragment.

It may never take form as a document but will be present in every thread of the tapestry that is your church. It will be in your values, culture and church ethics. It will be spoken of, loved and most importantly, protected. For this reason I am suggesting that the last term of our building agreement should be a commitment to protect it.

The final chapters of Nehemiah's story illustrate this. The people had entered an agreement to keep God's word and ways – the Law of Moses. It seems strange, then, that the document they produced also contained some specific things they were particularly promising to do – because all of them were already in the Law of Moses. So why repeat them?

The answer lies in their history. It was these requirements in particular that their forefathers had violated when they broke God's law. So they were making a doubly strong statement of intent. Out of interest, those three things were: not to intermarry with people from the surrounding nations, not to break the Sabbath, and not to neglect bringing their tithes and offerings to God's house.

In the years that followed, Nehemiah supervised the re-populating of the city and then returned to Persia for a period.

All the while he would have been getting reports of progress in Jerusalem. Then, some years later he returned to see the progress for himself.

He returned in the same frame of mind he had left with. To him the building agreement was still intact. He therefore returned still feeling what God felt, still totally committed to playing his part and still responding to God's word – just as, he expected, everyone else was. Sadly, he was disappointed. As he assessed the evolving situation in Jerusalem he discovered that despite the specific agreement they had all signed:

The house of God was being neglected

The tithes and offerings had diminished so that the Levites, who were supported by that income, had had to return to their fields. His response was: "I rebuked the officials and asked them, 'Why is the house of God neglected?' Then I called them together and stationed them at their posts" (Nehemiah 13:11). His rebuke was followed by immediate action to rectify things.

The Sabbath was being broken

People were openly trading on the Sabbath. His response was, "I rebuked the nobles of Judah and said to them, 'What is this wicked thing you are doing – desecrating the Sabbath day? ... I ordered the doors to be shut and not opened until the Sabbath was over. I stationed some of my own men at the gates so that no load could be brought in on the Sabbath day ... I warned them and said ... If you do this again, I will lay hands on you'" (Nehemiah 13:17-22). Again, his rebuke was followed by immediate action to rectify the situation.

Some had intermarried

To his dismay, some Israelites had taken foreign wives and "half of their children ... did not know how to speak the language of Judah"

(Nehemiah 13:24). What a disaster! His response was: "I rebuked them and called curses down on them. I beat some of the men and pulled out their hair. I made them take an oath in God's name and said: 'You are not to give your daughters in marriage to their sons, nor are you to take their daughters in marriage for your sons or for yourselves'" (Nehemiah 13:25). Pretty radical, but again, a rebuke followed by actions.

All this flowed from the heart of a man who was as passionate as ever about the building agreement they had. He was still feeling what God felt about things, still involved in the rebuilding and still responding to God's word. He had a zeal for the agreement, which motivated him to protect it fervently.

I believe that it's crucial for local church-building teams to have a similar determination to protect the "building agreement." Give one another permission to keep each other on track; speak the truth in love to one another; be your brother's keeper; teach and admonish one another from the reservoir of God's word that is in you. Be ready to stand up for our shared values and where necessary say, "Don't speak like that, it is ungodly" or, "Don't act like that, it gives all Christians a bad name." Urge one another to avoid the very appearance of evil and by so doing, protect the thing that holds you all together as fellow church-builders: your "building agreement."

There you have it. The first dynamic that keeps a church cohesive and holds it all together is your "building agreement."

Secret ingredient

There is a second principle that works to further strengthen the "glue" that holds your church together. This one is not often spoken about in the church today. It's become a bit like the "secret ingredient" in a recipe! Informed church-builders realise its importance but find it hard to communicate in a society where the rights of the individual are high on the agenda. What could it be? In a word: submission. Or more properly stated: mutual submission. How do we make a theme like mutual submission sound attractive when everything around us is saying, "Submit to no-one"? It's not easy but it is absolutely essential. For without a healthy understanding of biblical submission, the church will simply not hold together. Mutual submission, therefore, is not just glue, it is "super-glue"!

Submission is at the core of Christianity. It means accepting somebody else's authority or deferring to another's knowledge, judgment, or experience. And that is precisely what we did when we made Jesus Lord of our lives. We bowed the knee to him, gladly submitting to his benevolent rule. We happily acknowledge that we are no longer our own but have been bought with a price – and so we could go on with the biblical phraseology. I am sure you get my point.

One of the most wonderful descriptions of Christ in the Bible (Colossians 1:17) states: "In him all things hold together." That says it all. Jesus is the centre point. He holds it all together. And we hold together as a church only because we are each fully submitted to him.

He is the head of the body. Without submission to the head, as his body we have no mind, hearing, sight or voice. He is the Good Shepherd. Without submission to the shepherd we, his flock, remain lost, thirsty, hungry and in constant danger. So we could go on. It is all about Jesus. Submission to him is paramount. And as we each individually do so, it unites us around his purpose and releases us to play our part in it to the full.

Reverence for Christ

But that is usually not the problem. Churches do not generally fragment and fall apart because of a person's refusal to submit to Christ. Indeed, when churches split, or people leave a congregation, each party usually affirms they have "heard from God" and believe they are "following the Lord" in their going. And as long as that is true, damage to the wider body of Christ is minimized. We happily release one another with grace and stature, as we discussed earlier in this book.

The problem has more to do with our inability to work in a church-building team relationship with people we do not always get on with. All manner of personal idiosyncrasies, individual likes and dislikes, cultural preferences and personality clashes, get in the way of progress. And they can become the seeds of separation if left unattended.

It is, for example, difficult to sit and listen to someone preaching if you simply do not like them as a person. Separating between their role as "God's mouthpiece" and their annoying personality quirks is a challenge! And very often the human issues prevail, meaning we never really hear God's voice because we cannot see beyond the personality traits we dislike.

But if we all just gathered around people we liked – people like us – the church would be a monochrome place. Diversity is what makes the church such a great environment in which to live, work and grow. We need each other's differences, not our similarities, to fully express God to the world around us.

The answer to this dilemma is in Paul's teaching to the Ephesians. He tells them to "submit to one another out of reverence for Christ" (Ephesians 5:21). This is a very important command in this context. He tells us to accept someone else's authority or defer to their knowledge, judgment or experience "out of reverence for Christ." That means we have to look beyond the human to the divine in one another. I submit to you because I respect the work Jesus has done in you. I acknowledge the gifts he has given you, the authority he has given you, the knowledge he has given you and the journey he has taken you on. It is the work of Christ in you that I revere and submit to.

If we can, then, find a way to manage our personality or worldview differences, we can stay together as part of a cohesive church-building team. That may mean we rarely spend time together outside of certain church settings. But that is fine, because we have a mutual respect for the deposit of Christ in one another, and draw on that freely and fully as fellow-members of the team. You don't have to be best friends to build church together. It helps, but it is not essential. And the fact that you aren't should never be allowed to cloud your ability to "submit to one another out of reverence for Christ."

Mutual submission is, therefore, a life-giving attitude that keeps the church body together and functioning as a unified whole. It touches every relationship of church life, inter-personal ones, inter-departmental ones, and even inter-church ones.

At the start of this chapter we posed the question, "Why do churches start to unravel or fragment, even after having done all the things we discussed earlier in this book?" My broad answer is that it happens for lack of a building agreement, or because of a failure to exercise mutual submission – or both.

Building God's house is the most rewarding work available to God's people. It embraces every other vocation and role you have in life. You build as a plumber, doctor, farmer, home-maker, scientist, artist or politician, bringing all those experiences to enrich the church. You build as a mother, father, grandparent or child, adding those qualities to our shared life. You build as an apostle, pastor, minister of mercy, teacher, intercessor or miracle-worker, adding your spiritual gifts to the unique mix that constitutes the church you are co-building. The beauty of the building is related to the combination of all these things and more. How important, then, that we let nothing separate us from our fellow church-builders and agree to "submit to one another out of reverence for Christ." For only in him do all things hold together.

Epilogue

My prayer is that these reflections from my 30 years of church-building may help you to play your part in building a thriving church in your locality. It is what the world desperately needs.

There is a "church everyone wants to build," the one described in the pictures and actions of the New Testament, and I encourage you to aim for that. But along the way, work with God to clarify the design of the bespoke expression of God's house that your personal church-building efforts are constructing. Delight in its unique flavour, colour and singular ability to reach the people God has destined to add to your community. Then invest your life into building that church: the church God wants you to build.

From time to time we come across popular phrases that sound as if they should be in the Bible. And I want to leave you with one. Its essence is certainly in the Bible but not its actual words. For those we have to thank the script-writers of *Field of Dreams*, the 1989 movie featuring Kevin Costner.

In the story he dreams of turning a cornfield on his remote farm into a baseball field. But the challenges are many, not least working out where the paying spectators would come from. He is moved into action by the mysterious voice of long-dead baseball heroes who famously say: "If you build it, they will come."

That phrase has become the currency of many a modern church-builder. I hear it quoted all over the place as a statement of faith and intent. And there's nothing wrong with that if you really believe it is God's word to you.

Back in 2007 we used it at Abundant Life Church to creatively help our people see that part of the church-building process is to build for the people who are yet to arrive. Unless we build in extra capacity, in accordance with God's direction, we will end up building a place just for ourselves. And the church exists primarily for others. However, our ability to receive them when they do come demands that we be ready, which means building today in the light of tomorrow's increase. And that takes faith.

Church-building is a faith exercise from first to last. Only as we step out in obedience and build the church of our dreams will all we need for the task come to us. But I remain convinced that "If you build it, they will come."

- Noah built the ark, and the animals came.
- David built the kingdom, and mighty men came.
- Solomon built the temple, and further wisdom, riches and honour came.
- Daniel built a life based on God's ways rather than those of his captors, and governance came.
- Ezra rebuilt the temple, and Nehemiah came to complete the city and make other reforms.
- Jesus built a sinless life, freely laid it down, and lost sinners came – people like us!

The principle holds good. If we will build "it" – whatever that looks like for you in church-building terms – "they" will come. And those who come will be just who you need for the task.

Paul told the Corinthian church: "You are … God's building" and taught them that "Each one should be careful how he builds" (1 Corinthians 3:9-10). So, let's take his words to heart and build carefully.

Go and do the work of gathering "living stones" and skilfully build them together into a house that can rightfully be called the church: the house of the living God.

It is our life's work: building church.

Appendix:
Church Health Check

The purpose of this exercise is to stimulate a healthy discussion about aspects of the local church you are helping to build.

• **Part A** consists of questions designed to raise awareness of your church-building context. It is especially helpful if an objective observer, who may be less familiar with the church and its context, facilitates the exercise.

• **Part B** asks you to place a numerical value on aspects of your church life as a basis for discussion.

• **Part C** invites reflection and discussion of your findings.

Because there is no scientific way of measuring the responses you will give, it remains a totally subjective exercise. For that reason it is unfruitful to compare "scores" with other churches, as everyone is scoring themselves! Just be honest.

Repeating the exercise with the same people, after a chosen period, is the only way to assess any kind of perceived progress or decline.

Prayerfully assess each aspect of your church, with the single goal of building a thriving church in accordance with the vision, mission, culture and values God has vested in you.

Part A: Understanding the church-building context

1. How long has the church been in existence?

2. What is the church's vision?

3. What is the church's mission strategy?

4. What are the core values shaping the culture of the church?

5. What is the church's current structure?

6. What is the composition/demographic of the church?

7. Your strengths: What does the church do consistently well?

8. Your weaknesses: What does the church always struggle with?

Part B: Early Church Health Check

Read the following passages as an introduction to this exercise:

- Acts 2:42-47
- Acts 4:32-34
- Acts 5:11-16
- Acts 5: 42

In them we find 14 features of the vibrant and healthy New Testament church. Discuss each feature in turn and, as a group, allocate a score to each when comparing it to your own church on the following basis:

> 1 = Feature not present
>
> 2 = Feature is present but at a low level/quality/quantity/ frequency; you have to look hard to find it.
>
> 3 = Feature is present at an average level/quality/quantity/ frequency
>
> 4 = Feature is present and easy to locate across a significant proportion of the church/above average frequency
>
> 5 = Feature is ever present, across the whole church; you can't miss it!

For a fuller explanation of each feature, please refer to Chapter 3.

1. They were individually devoted – "They devoted themselves..." (Acts 2:42)

2. The Bible was read, taught and outworked – "They devoted themselves to...the apostles' teaching" (Acts 2:42).

3. They enjoyed fellowship with God and each other – "They devoted themselves to... fellowship" (Acts 2:42).

4. They broke bread regularly – "They devoted themselves to...the breaking of bread" (Acts 2:42)

5. They were a praying people – "They devoted themselves...to prayer" (Acts 2:42)

6. The supernatural was evident – "Everyone was filled with awe at the many wonders and signs performed by the apostles" (Acts 2:43; see also 5:12, 15-16).

7. They enjoyed togetherness and a shared life – "All the believers were together and had everything in common" (Acts 2:44).

8. They held large and small gatherings – "...in the temple courts and from house to house" (Acts 5:42).

9. They were a praising people – "They continued to meet together... praising God" (Acts 2:47)

10. They grew numerically – "More and more men and women believed in the Lord and were added to their number" (Acts 2:37, 5:14).

11. The fear of the Lord was present – "Everyone was filled with awe" (Acts 2:43; see also 5:13-14)

12. They taught and proclaimed the gospel – "They never stopped teaching and proclaiming the good news" (Acts 5:42).

13. They enjoyed the favour of the community – "Enjoying the favour of all the people" (Acts 2:47; see also 5:13).

14. They were a grace-filled community – "God's grace was so powerfully at work in them all" (Acts 4:33).

Part C: Discussion

1. How do you think you did?

- The maximum possible score = 70
- The average score = 42

2. How do you propose to strengthen the weaker features?

3. How will you ensure the strong features stay strong?

4. Are there any other significant changes you need to make as a result of this exercise?

References

1. Scanlon, Paul, *Crossing Over*, (Nelson Books, 2006)

2. Barnett, Tommy, *There's a Miracle in Your House* (Creation House, 1993)

3. Minear, Paul S., *New Testament Images of the Church*, (Westminster John Knox Press, 2004)

4. Warren, Rick, *The Purpose-Driven Church*, (Zondervan, 1995)

5. Buckingham, Marcus, and Clifton, Donald, *Now Discover Your Strengths*, (Pocket Books, 2005)

6. Maxwell, John, *Developing the Leader Within You*, (Thomas Nelson, 1993)

7. Groeschel, Craig, *IT*, (Zondervan, 2008)

8. Gerald, Kevin, *Design or Default* (Nelson Books, 2006)

9. Hybels, Bill, *The Volunteer Revolution* (Zondervan, 2004)

10. Hybels, Bill, *Courageous Leadership* (Zondervan, 2002)

Further Information

For details of other teaching resources and
the ministry of Stephen Matthew please visit:

website: www.stephenmatthew.com

twitter.com/StephenMatthew_

facebook.com/pastorstephenmatthew

The Abundant Life Church:
www.alm.org.uk